The Wanderers

The Wanderers

Henry A. Garon

ORBIS BOOKS
Maryknoll, New York 10545

Founded in 1970, Orbis Books endeavors to publish works that enlighten the mind, nourish the spirit, and challenge the conscience. The publishing arm of the Maryknoll Fathers and Brothers, Orbis seeks to explore the global dimensions of the Christian faith and mission, to invite dialogue with diverse cultures and religious traditions, and to serve the cause of reconciliation and peace. The books published reflect the views of their authors and do not represent the official position of the Maryknoll Society. To learn more about Maryknoll and Orbis Books, please visit our website at www.maryknollsociety.org.

Published by Orbis Books, Maryknoll, New York 10545-0308.
Manufactured in the United States of America.

Library of Congress Cataloging-in-Publication Data

Garon, Henry A.
  The wanderers / Henry A. Garon.
    p. cm.
  ISBN 978-1-57075-820-1 (pbk.)
  1. Poverty—Religious aspects—Christianity. 2. Homelessness—Religious aspects—Christianity. 3. Poor. 4. Homeless persons. 5. Church work with the poor. 6. Church work with the homeless. I. Title.
  BV4647.P6G37 2009
  261.8'325—dc22
                                        2008038399

CONTENTS

ACKNOWLEDGMENTS

The writer wishes to acknowledge the kind assistance given him by Rev. Henry Engelbrecht, Rev. Ignatius Roppollo, and Sr. Alma Marie Tivenan, SBS, who served as readers, and by Marie R. Garon, whose final editing of the stories helped greatly. Others whose names are mentioned within the textual accounts themselves also helped.

INTRODUCTION

If you live in an urban area, it's likely that you have been approached by certain people of the streets. Sometimes they seem to appear from out of nowhere, such as when you've stopped to fill your tank at a self-serve gasoline station. At other times they'll just come right up to you on the sidewalk and start talking.

Most of us find that our guard usually goes up when a slovenly dressed stranger approaches us, especially in an isolated place. What if the person has a scheme to rob or assault us? And ethical questions quickly arise: Am I obligated to help such persons? Ought I to give them money? To what extent do I owe it to my family to avoid such people out of concern for my personal safety?

Street persons sometimes break the ice by approaching with cheerful greetings. They have a way of sizing up people very quickly. They begin with a friendly "Good morning" or "How are you today?" If a person responds in the slightest way to their greeting, they usually say that they have a question to ask, and one need not be a genius to know what they have in mind.

I dislike this practice of theirs, of waiting for me to stop and alight from my vehicle, then approaching me for money, as they often say, "to buy something to eat." Rarely do I give them money. If food is available nearby, I prefer to buy a sandwich, give it to them, wish them well, and depart. Often my wife and I carry cheese crackers and a can or two of potted meat or Vienna sausages in our car, something nourishing and easily opened by means of a pull-tab, and we give a can or two to persons who seek money for food.

Yet, as I have discovered, money is not necessarily the main thing such people are looking for. Some want simply to be heard and encouraged, to feel that they have made a connection with someone who is willing to listen. Thus, this book is also about listening—listening not only to the wanderers of society but also to our inner selves. I must listen to my inner self, question and discern my motives. I must know my capabilities and face my limitations and decide what I can do and how I ought to serve. I must do these things if I am to explore who I am in this world, if I am to know something positive regarding my own definition.

I shall begin by writing interchangeably of both "street people" and "the homeless," allowing distinctions between the two terms to come to light later. I write as one who has been trained to listen to them, to hear with the so-called third ear, to lead them on in a client-centered counseling style designed to encourage them to talk about their pains, their frustrations, and their resentments. My task differs somewhat from those of professional social workers insofar as I do it within the context of crisis counseling in a part-time ministry as a deacon in my church.

I am a recently retired professor of physics, a person who has spent thirty-nine years teaching, captivated by the experience of having explained the workings of the world to more than nine thousand college students. I am also the husband of a very fine lady, and the father of four wonderful children, one of whom we recently lost by way of an automobile mishap.

Why, then, do I engage in a ministry with street people? In truth, it is because I do not want to know myself forever as a person who passed through this one and only life on earth associating solely with the fortunate ones of society. Psychologically, I wish to know myself as expansive and inclusive. The central consideration is that one day long ago Jesus Christ said that whatever we do for his least brethren, we do

for him. I happen to believe those words of his. I take them
literally and have concluded that I ought to do something at
least slightly radical toward finding him in those whom the
world considers lowest and least.

The stories in this book are true. They focus on people
who roam our streets. The stories tell of who these people are,
where they come from, how they survive, and what they have
and do not have on their minds. I relate the stories for readers who wish to "tune in" to the homeless, who want to better understand the driving forces behind their oft-bewildering
lifestyles.

The stories are presented from a Christian perspective, in
particular from that of a Catholic permanent deacon, and they
"wonder aloud" about what might be done to improve the
plight of the homeless. The stories I tell here span the twenty-
eight-year period during which I have been ministering to the
homeless one night a week. Over this period, and especially in
more recent years, I have seen changes and improvements in
the types of services offered to the homeless. There are some
things that have not changed, however, and they include the
problems—alcohol and addictions, abuse and mental illness—
that continue to plague people who live on the streets.

I have avoided using the real names of street persons and,
in most cases, the names of the cities from which they came.
My work with the homeless has made it necessary for me to
grapple with some questions and problems of my own. In
these pages I reveal what some of these questions and problems were and describe how I have—at least to some extent—
resolved them.

The setting for these stories is Ozanam Inn, a refuge for
street men at 843 Camp Street in New Orleans. Women and
children also come there for meals, but cannot be accommodated overnight. Ozanam Inn is owned by the St. Vincent de
Paul Society and is operated under the supervision of the
Catholic Archdiocese of New Orleans. The Inn has been in
operation for more than fifty years.

As these stories unfold, I relate how I and others meet these wandering people without endangering ourselves. I focus on what we do for them and what they do for us. And I hope that you, my reader, will derive some insights into their world, a realm far removed from that of those who live and thrive in fast-moving America, the land of dreams that generally come true for those who persistently keep their sails to the wind while remaining sober.

1

MINISTERING TO WANDERERS

I am usually tired but relaxed when I get to Ozanam Inn by late afternoon. I sometimes hold small gatherings for the purpose of allowing the men to vent their frustrations, or I read and explain certain biblical passages to them. However, one must not assume that street persons are in a relaxed mood.

Jeff was first to arrive for a gathering one evening. Staring at the floor, he slowly shuffled in, looking depressed and exhausted.

"I just got out of Charity Hospital," he said in a quiet and matter-of-fact manner. "It was four shots that I got."

Misunderstanding him, and assuming that he was referring to having received medical shots—injections—at the hospital, I asked naively, "What were the shots for?"

"I don't know!" he responded. "I have no idea why they hate me!"

"Wait a minute—" I said. "You mean to say that you were shot with a gun and not with a hypodermic syringe?"

"Yeah, with a gun! Last week!"

Pulling up his sleeve, he showed me his arm, which was covered with bandages, and he said, "It happened when I went into my apartment building two nights ago. The hall was dark. As I made my way toward the light switch, I heard a voice say, 'Don't move!' Then there were more voices. There must have been three other people there. So I ran toward the window at the far end of the hall. They began shooting at me. It sounded as if they were passing the gun around, each one taking his turn shooting while scolding the others for missing me. They hit me four times in the dark, but none of the hits were serious. They grazed my side and got me in my arm and my shoulder."

"Did you get a look at any of these people?" I asked.

"No, I only heard them. I zigged and I zagged and got out of there as quick as I could. I was hurting real bad and, man, did they sound mean!"

He went on to say how afraid he has become of the dark, how he keeps imagining all kinds of dangers, how he finds it difficult to fall asleep at night. And the darkly etched circles under his eyes seemed to verify his every word.

"Were those guys ever caught?" I asked.

"No, they got away. I was too busy getting myself to the hospital to worry about having them caught. I have no idea who they were. For all I know, they might be sleeping right here in this dormitory tonight. Right here at Ozanam!"

When I got home that night I related Jeff's story to my wife. Marie has always been supportive of my work with street people.

"You know," she said, "It really makes you think, doesn't it? Here we are, safe in our house. We go to bed at night feeling quite secure. With bars on our windows, automatic flood lamps and motion sensors outside our home, we can sleep in peace. It's easy to forget how some other people can't enjoy even ordinary freedom from fear at night."

The Name Ozanam

Ozanam Inn is named after Frederick Ozanam, a philosophy professor at the Sorbonne in Paris during the "top hat and frock coat" era of the early 1800s. It is said that Ozanam felt compelled to refute another philosophy professor who was attacking the church.

Once he had started refuting his colleague, he discovered—to his dismay—that a student movement was beginning to form around him. He felt as if he were being coerced into taking a leadership role in the movement. Gradually, his opponent softened his stand and moved closer to Ozanam's point of view.

Ozanam eventually married a woman named Amelie and the couple had a daughter. One day an incident occurred that radically changed his life. Ozanam was debating with several students, emphasizing how the principles of Christ had enabled the church to do great works and triumph over pagan philosophies. Then one of the students challenged him.

"You talk about the great works of the church in the past. But what about today?" the student asked.

"Haven't you seen all the works of charity around you today?" Ozanam retorted. "Look at the orphanages! Look at the hospitals!"

"Yes, but you laypeople seem to put all of the burden for helping the poor on your clergy and religious. Don't try to impress us with what your priests and nuns are doing for the poor. What about you, Frederick Ozanam? What are you personally doing for the poor?"

The outcome of that challenge was that Ozanam and his students organized a small "conference of charity" that gradually grew into the St. Vincent de Paul Society. Although Ozanam died at age forty, his Society continued to expand. Currently it has 750,000 members in 112 nations throughout the world. In 1997 Frederick Ozanam was given the title "Blessed" by Pope John Paul II. It is hoped by many that in time he will be elevated to sainthood.

Receiving the Homeless

A recent survey has shown that the number of homeless in America is estimated to be in excess of three million and increasing. In speaking of "the homeless," we refer to people who, for whatever reasons, have no regular place of residence.

However, we must be careful when using the word "home-less," because many people do not appreciate being known by this term.

"I'm not a homeless man—the world is my home!" one man boasted. "Everywhere I go I'm at home! I don't have to live in a big house like most people do just because people think I ought to. I'm a nature person!" he insisted, and then he added, "How would you like it if I called you a 'boxed-in' person because you live in a house?"

As newcomers in the world of the homeless back in 1980, Ron and I were asked to help register street people as they arrived for a night's rest at the Inn. City and state regulations similar to those applicable to hotels and motels had to be met. All overnight guests were expected to have some form of identification. As Ron and I sat at the registration desk to record names, we spoke briefly with each person. From our standpoint, this procedure was good in the sense that it gave us a chance to "break the ice," to be on speaking terms with each of these men before encountering them later in the dormitory.

Wanderers of every type come to Ozanam Inn—the big and the little, the clean-shaven, the bearded, the healthy, the sick, the friendly and outgoing, the silent and sullen, the tense, the stiff-legged and the loose-jointed, the apparently clean and the definitely dirty, some covered with ugly-looking tattoos. And, O God, how some of them smell! You can tell from a distance who these people are by the no-man's-land that encircles them. Regardless of their arrival time, they have trouble standing in line because their peers banish them all the way to the end of the line and even beyond.

Some of the people look terrible when they come into the building. But, after they have taken a shower and eaten a sandwich, their spirits seem to lift. They become more willing to speak. Those who are open to conversation are often rec-ognizable by the way they look us in the eye when we walk past them.

Ground Rules

Ron and I first met while taking part in the formation program for becoming permanent deacons. Following three years of academic and spiritual training, we took a clinical pastoral education course that prepared us for working in hospitals, prisons, and hospices.

Toward the end of our training, the two of us were assigned to work with street people at Ozanam Inn. Our mentors, Hilton and Bernie, gave us good advice: "Remember that you are going among the suffering primarily as a listener. Your task is to get troubled persons to talk about their pains, their frustrations, their resentments. You want to get them to vent, if possible, to 'let off steam' and rid themselves of tensions they experience, even in the form of urges to kill. Get them to do that, if for no reason other than the fact that it is good for them. Express agreement with them whenever you can, asking questions here and there to keep the conversation going. Guide them toward seeing their troubles, leading them to the point of discovering what they ought to do for themselves. Finally, have them pray with you, if you can. But always keep the focus on them. Say nothing about yourself unless you must. Even then, make such comments very brief. You are there to help others rise from their anger and depression, not to impress them with your eloquence and brilliant accomplishments."

As newcomers at Ozanam, Ron and I quickly discovered that ministering to street people was very different from engagement in parish work. Our presence at Ozanam was very clearly in harmony with the intentions of the Second Vatican Council, which had decided to ordain men, both married and single, as permanent deacons that they might go out into the marketplace and serve the needy.

Following a brief familiarization period, Steven Taylor, Ozanam's director, allowed Ron and me to conduct the initial briefing session, a ritual of sorts that takes place on the ground floor prior to the admittance of new men to the third-floor dormitory.

After the newcomers had been processed, they were gathered into a group. I then addressed them and said: "Good evening, gentlemen! My name is Deacon Henry, and we welcome you to Ozanam Inn. We hope that you will have a very good night. I want to let you know how things work here, and how we will get you as quickly as possible into the dormitory room where you can take a shower and enjoy a clean bed. You are expected to have some form of identification. If you don't have identification, you'll be able to stay only one night here at Ozanam. Please ask us and we will tell you how to obtain an ID card if you need one.

"We will also give you a card of our own that entitles you to stay here free of charge up to seven nights a year. Some of you may have valuables that you will want to check in. You can drop them into one of those big brown envelopes over there. We will write your name and social security number on the envelope. All the envelopes will be locked away for the night and your valuables will be given back to you in the morning when you leave.

"No one is allowed to take luggage upstairs. All luggage must be checked in before you enter the dorm. We will need to inspect anything (such as books, magazines, or medicines) you might want to take upstairs. As you enter the third-floor dorm, a worker up there will check you in. He will give you a towel and pajamas and assign you a bed. You must take a shower and wear the pajamas we give you. No one is allowed to sit on his bed in street clothes. As you leave in the morning, we will expect you to return the towel and pajamas to us.

"Remember that smoking is not allowed in the sleeping area. You can, if you wish, smoke in the rest room, but only in the rest room. You will find a large sign on its door reading:

SMOKING IN HERE ONLY! Anyone found smoking in the dorm will be immediately put out of this place! There are no exceptions to this rule because it has to do with safety—it is intended to avoid the risk of fire.

"Other prohibited actions include drinking liquor, harassing or bullying another person, or making sexual advances with or without the consent of another. Anyone doing any of these things will immediately be permanently expelled.

"You will be awakened at 5:30 and called down to breakfast at 6. As you leave after breakfast, you will be given the belongings you checked in. You may, if you wish, return here for a dinner at 2:30 in the afternoon."

Food for the Homeless

The staff at Ozanam operates two vans that go out daily to collect food. Meats such as sausages and ground beef are especially desired. Donors include hotels, restaurants, ships in dock, and grocery stores. They have various types of food which, while possibly past its "sell-by" date, is nevertheless suitable for eating if consumed within a few days.

Steven, who often drives the food van, relates the following: "What I love about New Orleans is family-owned businesses whose owners have a sense of responsibility toward the community. Many are willing to immediately make food donations. In certain other cities, by contrast, everything seems to be owned by conglomerates. When we go to them and ask for leftovers, some say, 'Well, we must first write to our home office and ask for their permission.'

"Others say, 'If we allow you to have it, then we would have to give it to others!' Once a businessman explained: 'We used to give food for the homeless until a man who ate one of our sandwiches got sick. A lawyer, on his behalf, sued us for half-a-million dollars!'

"In effect, then, certain large firms and stock-owned establishments tell us: 'We'd love to help you but...' Thus, we generally send our vans to the smaller businesses to collect food. The smaller donors are very important to us."

Hilbert and "The Crew"

Hilbert came to Ozanam dispossessed of wallet, satchel, and the ends of two fingers on his left hand. The wallet had been taken away from him by a bully. His satchel had disappeared after he had left it near a lavatory while using the toilet. And he spoke of losing his fingers in a drafty house near Erie, Pennsylvania, where he experienced the terrible bite of an unusually severe winter. He explained how a surgeon, a "really nice fellow," amputated the ends of his fingers, as he said, "in order to save the rest."

Hilbert had grown up on a farm, and so he knew the meaning of work. Recognizing his willingness to work, the staff at Ozanam accepted him as part of "the crew," as it is called.

In the workings of Ozanam Inn certain street men, by virtue of their skills and earnestness, are retained as members of the crew, a team of temporary workers who help operate the facility. Crew members enjoy the use of special dormitories, one for day workers, another for night workers. Duties of crew members include sweeping and mopping, answering telephones, running errands, preparing and cooking meals, washing, sorting, and folding clothes, making up beds, washing dishes, painting, and repair work. The typical stay of a crewman at the Inn is about four months, after which he is expected to move on and work toward further improving his life. Such was the case with Hilbert. I saw him weekly for about four months. Then he disappeared and I never laid eyes on him again.

Lady in the Shadows

While returning home one night, I paused at a filling station, filled the gas tank, and paid the cashier. As I was walking back toward my car, a voice called from out of the shadows.

"Mister, can you spare me a dollar?"

I turned around and saw an elderly black woman. Dressed in dark clothes, she was hidden among the shrubs, seated on a ledge between two or three large supermarket-type paper bags. So I lingered a moment to speak.

"You have no place to stay?" I asked.

"No, sir. I lost my husband years ago. So I lived with my sister in the St. Thomas project. But she died three months ago. Now I have no place to stay."

"Well, how do you make it? Where do you sleep and eat and bathe?"

"I just go from one place to another place with my bags of clothes," she said. "I use the ladies room in filling stations. I can take care of my needs there and wash myself a little. I ask people for money and I buy myself food and wash my clothes in a launderette."

"How do you get your sleep and rest?" I asked.

"I take myself a nap here and there, mostly in the day time. I find a little place where nobody will do me harm. I sit there for a time, and if nobody shoos me away, I just lean back and take me my nap. At night I come to places like this that's well lit up. And I ask people for money.

"I'm careful with the money they give me," she continued. "I keep away from people who might steal it from me. I buy my food and save the rest. Every time I save twenty dollars, I go to a little hotel and rent a room. I do that about twice a week. When I get there I take me a nice warm bath. Then I fall into bed and I really, really go to sleep. I get to feeling good once again! And then the next day I go back on the street."

In cases such as this, I do indeed give money on the spot and consider it well spent.

The Importance of Early Training

Often a lack of good early training is at the root of the problems of street people. And it can be at the root of some problems of other people too.

One day a roving man, an acquaintance of ours whom we had earlier met through a friend, knocked at our door. Before my wife or I could answer, our small children had recognized him and let him in. We found him settled comfortably in our living room, seated in a chair from which there was a clear view of our bedroom and bathroom.

"Please do not walk into our house until my wife or I let you in," I said to him.

He refused to acknowledge that his behavior might have been problematic or his ways offensive.

"Why the hell don't you teach your children not to let people in until you come to the door?" was his response.

He was, indeed, to some extent correct. And so my wife and I did in fact afterwards follow his suggestion by impressing on our children the importance of calling us to the door before opening it.

Telling Him the Truth

They called him Toledo. He was a man of about fifty to whom I brought food on several occasions pending the arrival of the first of his welfare checks.

Toledo was an outspoken nonconformist by nature and spoke of having once encouraged revolution in America. I suggested that he visit Ozanam Inn for wholesome meals, an idea he seemed to shun as something below his dignity. Immediately, he informed me of his ancestry and of the noble profession of his father in years gone by. He made it very clear that he did not wish to associate with street people.

Each week my wife, my parishioners, and I would provide him with limited help in the form of canned food and small amounts of money which I delivered to him after work on Fridays.

Then his checks began to arrive. Still, he wanted me to continue bringing him food. I did this, but in decreasing amounts while he paid off some of his debts. Finally one day he said to me: "I sure like those canned goods you bring me. They help me a lot. I have enough now to give some of them away to people. I can keep on the good side of my landlord by giving him those cans of tuna fish you bring me. He feeds his cats with that."

We decided to stop providing him with food, and, as expected, he became angry at my wife and me for this. He insulted us harshly over the telephone, hung up on us, and ceased calling us for a time.

About a month later he called. "Can you help me?" he asked. "I'm standing out here next to Jesuit High School. I lost my glasses and I can hardly find my way around. And I'm hungry!"

I jumped into my car and drove to Banks Street where I spotted him sitting on the steps of the school. He was obviously on the verge of being arrested, for across the street stood two policemen watching his every move. I parked and walked up to him. On seeing me lead him away from the school, the policemen immediately departed. I drove him to a fast-food place where he stuffed himself on hamburgers and milk shakes. I also purchased an extra burger for him to take along with him. Then I drove him over to Notre Dame Seminary where he had stored his belongings in a grocery shopping cart parked beneath an oak tree in front of the building.

I was amazed at his belongings. In addition to several blankets, he had an accumulation of two weeks' worth of newspapers, two thick telephone books, and a ten-inch-thick pile of magazines.

"Toledo, why do you carry all this heavy stuff around?" I asked. "It must weigh at least fifty pounds, and it pulls on you wherever you go."

"Well, I need something to read. You're looking at my reading materials," he said.

"My gosh, man! You don't need to lug all of that stuff around. You can find telephone books at telephone booths. And if you want to read magazines, all you have to do is drop in at a library. You're a citizen, you know! Public libraries must let you in as long as you keep yourself halfway decent."

"Yeah, I know," he said. But there's nothing like having your own books to read."

Then he regressed into silence. A minute or so later he began speaking again—now on a different subject.

"Henry," he said, "It's too bad you don't have an apartment in your back yard where I could live."

"You think so?" I asked.

"Yeah! You know, Henry, all I need is a little love."

"That's true," I replied. "But do you have any idea of how difficult you make it for people to be drawn to you?"

"What do you mean?" he asked.

I decided to level with him in homespun terms, for there were unpleasant things he needed to hear.

"Look, Toledo, you have a college degree but you don't know how to listen." I said. "You are demanding and self-righteous, boiling with anger from out of the past when you preached revolution in the 1960s! You visualize yourself as a liberator of the oppressed. Where are your revolutionary friends today? They're gone! None of them even bothers to keep in touch with you. Twenty-two years have slipped by and you're still full of resentments! All you do is hang around idle all day and blabber your mouth. Not only do you interrupt others who talk with you, but you interrupt even yourself while you're talking. While speaking of one thing you recall a different thing and switch over to that new subject. Do you have any idea of how difficult you make it for people to listen to you?" I asked.

"Yeah, yeah, I know. There's a lot of people who don't like me, including even my relatives. Nobody seems to understand me. That's because I'm neurotic, Henry."

"Okay, I agree. You're neurotic. That's a fact of life. But what do you intend to do about it? Now that you know what's wrong, how are you going to manage it?" I asked.

He, of course, was unable to formulate a workable plan. Persons with serious neuroses seldom can. And so, the conversation ended. Nevertheless, I felt better for having told him the truth as I saw it. The fact that I had leveled with him seemed to help our relationship. Part of his problem seemed to have stemmed from the fact that nobody had ever really been honest with him, and that he had never been taught how to relate to others.

Several months after this conversation my wife and I heard, quite by accident, that Toledo had suffered a heart attack and passed away.

"Well, he's probably at peace now," said my wife.

"I sure hope so," I responded, while saying a silent prayer for him.

Balancing Commitments to Ministry and Family

As a permanent deacon I am, indeed, a member of the Catholic clergy. As a married man, however, my first duty under God is to my family, and, while I was still teaching, to my employer who provided me with the means of supporting my family. Therefore, my ministry to street people has been of necessity different from that of celibates who have no immediate family commitments. Were I one of them I would be free to respond favorably to telephone calls from troubled persons late at night and into the pre-dawn hours. But I must also consider my family and my other commitments. Especially when I was teaching, for example, I needed my sleep in order to be mentally sharp in the classroom the following morning. Therefore, I have not encouraged troubled persons to phone me at home. I prefer to go out and meet them away from my home and family.

Indeed, it has happened that a mentally deficient person has put my wife and me to the test. A man we knew phoned us twice one night, telling us how lonely he was, wanting us to bring him books so that he might read. Another called after midnight, insisting that he was about to die, declaring that night to be his last on earth. He demanded that I visit him immediately. Having become familiar with his attacks of depression, I refused, although I did promise to bring his needs to the attention of his pastor in the morning. Not surprisingly, the man did not die that night.

One day, on learning that I was a professor, a man of the streets inquired where I taught. I told him the name of my university. At one o'clock on an autumn afternoon he showed up unannounced in my office and made a nuisance of himself during a time when students were knocking at my door to see me about assignments. He sat in my office, reading something or other taken from my bookshelf and frequently interrupted my conversations with my students. I finally asked him to leave. He left, but not before chiding me for allying myself with what he called "the establishment."

Needless to say, I thenceforth ceased allowing street persons to visit my office on campus.

In time, I also learned that it was best almost never to speak about my private life with street people, my primary reason being that I wish to shield my family from possible harm or harassment. At the Inn I introduce myself simply as Deacon Henry. It bothers me that a demented or criminal person might search me out in my neighborhood, or insist on being received at "the home of the deacon" as if it were a parish rectory or refuge of a sort. Indeed, there are wonderful persons among street people; however, I know for certain that con artists and amoral persons do navigate among them. I reflect on the Christian call to take in strangers: "Do not neglect to show hospitality to strangers, for by doing that some have entertained angels without knowing it" (Hebrews 13:2).

I somehow wish that I could follow those words literally, but it would be unfair to my family were I to attempt to do so in today's world. Early on I resolved not to expect my wife and children to engage in helping the unfortunates in the same way that I help them, for my weekly visits to Ozanam are my response to an inner call that is my own and not necessarily that of my family.

The Limits to What We Can Give

Among the unfortunates are many who, for one reason or other, seem unable to methodically begin something of permanence. They worry much and putter without end. Sometimes sitting on the steps and spitting on the sidewalk seem to constitute their idea of operating at peak efficiency. Referring to work, they speak as if their job is one of simply holding out, awaiting the arrival of "the big opportunity." Some refuse to perform certain tasks which they imagine to be beneath their dignity.

Years go by and they find themselves surviving without employment. Whereas some speak of immediate creative activities, these deeply afflicted unfortunates can only rehash the past. Those of them who are in need of live listeners boast about the places they've been during their heyday, or the books they've read. Searching for recognition, they mention the schools they attended, the times when they had it rough, the tonnage of the ships they once piloted. Some are chronically given to distraction and, therefore, cannot persist for long in any task. Days turn into months as they watch the coming and going of time. Theirs is a life of trivialities which they cover up and conceal, often with endless big talk. They pause from their idleness to have a smoke, then proceed to philosophize about a poor economy or the current do-nothing government administration.

I once invited such a man (who declared himself to be a recovered alcoholic) to go with me on a day-long trip I was about to undertake for the purpose of renovating a house in the country. He seemed enthusiastic about my invitation, mentioning that he was looking forward to helping me work. When we arrived at the site, I assigned him a light task—cleaning windows—while I busied myself sanding floors. He worked on the windows for about ten minutes, then began to joke and tell tales about far-flung places he had visited. Repeatedly he paused to take breaks. He philosophized, speculated, and jabbered to the point of distracting my young son who had come along to help. In the end, I had to find ways of coaxing the man to take walks so as to leave us alone so that we could get some work done. It became obvious to me then that psychologically he was unfit for work. He found no meaning in routine tasks. It was then that I also realized that motivation is perhaps something one can't give to another person; it has to come from within.

2

THE WALKING WOUNDED

Steven Taylor, Ozanam's director, recalled words from a workshop in Albuquerque for people who work with the wanderers of society, words spoken by a physician who heads New York's work with street people:

> Ladies and gentlemen, let me tell you something. If you are perfectly sound of mind and you go out on the streets to live, I promise that within six months you will no longer be sound and healthy of mind. This is because street life itself—concern for where you are going to stay, what's going to happen to you, where your next meal will come from, and your very safety—has such a strong emotional impact on you that after six months you will no longer be healthy mentally or emotionally.

Alcoholic Ministers

I had often heard that no profession is immune from the threat of alcoholism. The truth of this became evident to me one evening as I sat speaking to a small group. I suddenly became aware that one of the men in the group was probably a priest. What tipped me off was the fact that when speaking he used certain expressions I had heard decades before in a seminary, expressions such as "intrinsically good," "the Sacred Heart of Jesus," and certain Latin phrases.

In appearance, this man seemed to be cleaner and neater than most street persons. By the time the meeting ended he seemed to understand that I had recognized him as a priest. Nevertheless, I avoided speaking to him as if he had problems. Undoubtedly, he had a far better understanding of his problems than I. I felt that simply being with him and having him in our discussion was a privilege. We shook hands warmly as he left and I never saw him again. One can only speculate over the good that such a man, probably an alcoholic, might accomplish among street people.

When I related this to Steven, he told me that incidents like this were not unusual. As a matter of fact, he said, Brother Matthias in Albuquerque seemed to have an uncanny ability to spot former priests among street people. It is said that he once called aside a man who was waiting in line to eat.

"Come with me," he said. "I want to talk with you."

The man followed him into the office.

"How long have you been out of the priesthood?" the brother asked.

The startled man admitted that he had, indeed, been a priest.

Steven continued as follows: "I myself once met a man who told me he had been a priest. I fully believed him, as his compassionate manner and the words and phrases he used seemed to confirm his story. He said he had left his religious community ten years earlier, and that he was now interested in coming back into the active ministry. He asked me to arrange a meeting between him and a representative of the archdiocese, which I did. He agreed to return to Ozanam Inn the following evening for the purpose of confirming the meeting time. I called the chancery office and arranged a possible time for an appointment. Sad to say, the gentleman did not show up the next night, or the night after that, and we never saw him again."

Turning Off "The Switch"

Terry was a likable chap. Strong, with a ruddy complexion and sandy-blond hair, he spoke of having grown up in dry and barren lands out West where coyotes, rattlesnakes, and roadrunners "ruled the plains," as he said. He loved that country, but he needed a higher income. Ablaze with plans for moving up the ladder of success, he signed up for a truck-driver course. Not long afterwards he found himself behind the controls of an eighteen-wheeler that took him all over the country.

A year later in Alabama he ran into trouble, first with his truckdriver friends and later with the law. For Terry, having a single drink set him on a journey of no return. The accident he got into lost him his job and his freedom for more than five years. Every word he used when describing that unfortunate event was uttered with deep regret.

Terry longed to return to his native state and work his way up to owning a trucking business of his own, something on a smaller scale that he could handle without venturing far from home. The fact that he possessed a sense of wonder made me feel that his chances of succeeding in the future were probably very good.

"I don't drink anymore," he said to me. "I haven't touched a drop since my accident. Do you know how it feels to be an alcoholic?" he asked.

"I don't think so, Terry. Would you care to tell me?"

"Well, you see, ordinary people, when they are drinking, they quit whenever they sense that they have had enough. It's as if they can turn off an electric switch that goes to a motor inside them that makes them drink. But it's not like that with me. I can't even reach for the switch that turns my drinking motor off. It's like I don't even have such a switch. Once I start, there's no way I can stop. The only way that works with me is never to start. I can't afford ever to touch the stuff again for the rest of my life!"

A Stolen Treasure

People who are broken in spirit can easily become actors— masquerading, telling contradictory stories, sometimes seeming to speak different languages at different times. I came to this realization one night as I left the Inn and walked toward my car. A man filled with bottled cheer came staggering toward us, holding the half-empty bottle high above his head. His handsome features reminded me of the British actor Richard Burton.

"This is the best stuff in the world!" he loudly exclaimed. "This will take away your troubles any time, any day, any night," he added, while gesturing grandly at several other street persons who were present and who smilingly nodded in response.

Slowly, he continued to walk toward me. I felt uneasy about what he might do to me, but I held my ground. He placed his arms around my neck as if wanting to hug me, his bottle pressed against the side of my shoulder. Then he whispered in my ear.

"You have no idea how miserable I am! God, I am miserable! How I long to leave this earth! Pray for me, sir! Oh, God, take away my soul and bring it to heaven with you!"

Smiling, he backed away and left me even more quickly than he had approached. Down the street he ambled, bottle in hand, turning into an alley littered with empty beer cans and discarded cardboard boxes, a wreck of a scene that seemed to match the man's own inner life. I never saw him again. My total contact with him lasted no more than two minutes.

My pain at seeing this man's condition—his need to pretend, in particular—haunts me to this day. I can't help but picture him as he might have been had he been a healthy citizen—handsome, clean-shaven, well spoken, perhaps an insurance executive or a high-school principal, a good husband and father. What a loss to society, what a treasure stolen by his addiction!

Reason for Going to Church

Amidst the horrors of alcoholism and other addictions, how good it is to hear an addict admit to addiction. Such an admission brings the truth of the addiction into the light. And always, the embracing of truth is a necessary first step toward freedom.

The homeless need to hear that they are truly of worth, that God is truly in love with them. They must never be allowed to engage in thinking of themselves as worthless. Whereas it is legitimate for them to visualize themselves (and, indeed, all of humanity) as sinners and, therefore, weak and in need of forgiveness, they must never view themselves as evil. For, once they accept themselves as evil, from that moment on they are likely to engage in evil self-expression.

One day, a man at the Inn sat down beside me. His garments seemed to be an accumulation of holes surrounded by cloth. The odor of his breath was like that of a distillery. He began a story about a former lifestyle of his in which he set out for work before dawn and trudged home after dark. He made an honorable living raising frogs for restaurants. I told him of how my father had made his living by raising honeybees, and he seemed to enjoy hearing about that.

"I still go to church," he boasted. "Even though I'm drunk at times, I still go to church. And the reason why I go is because I know that something special is going on there, and I want to draw other people into going there! I figure that the word of the Lord is there. And if they see me going, then they, too, might want to go."

I had never thought of it that way, in terms of drunkards going to church to attract others toward church. It struck me that even sober persons who go to church seldom do so with the intention of encouraging others. Might it have been that the alcoholic was teaching me something new about motivation for attending church services?

Word Gets Out Fast

Some of the homeless behave very badly because in the streets there is a mixed community of souls, many of whom are not easy to relate to. When working with them, one must be ready to take some flak. On one occasion, a drunken man showed up at the Inn at meal time.

"I'm sorry, sir," Steven said. "We do not allow intoxicated persons to enter the dining hall. We'll give you a bag lunch, however, and you can sit on that outside bench and eat a sandwich there if you wish." But the man insisted on entering the dining room and eating what everybody else was eating. Steve quietly stood his ground.

"Do you realize where I come from?" the man asked. "I just walked in to New Orleans from Houston, and I haven't eaten since leaving Houston."

"Oh, really," Steven responded. "Houston is quite far, over three hundred miles away, and it must have taken you a full week to do that."

"That's right," the man responded. "And I'm not lying. I haven't eaten in a week!"

Realizing that he was getting nowhere, the man then changed his tactics.

"You're prejudiced!" he insisted. "You don't like black people! That's the only reason I can figure that you won't let me into the dining room!"

Steven told him to look inside the dining room and pointed out the numerous African-American people eating there.

"You know what the difference between you and them is?" Steven asked. "They're sober and you're not. That's why you're not coming into the dining room."

The man finally relented and accepted our bag lunch.

When Steven told me this story he said, "I don't think I was overly rigid with that man and I don't think I'm overly rigid with others like him. If they look as if they can halfway handle themselves, I allow them to enter. Were drunken men to enter, we would run certain risks. For example, they might slip in the shower and get a concussion. We took in a drunken man by mistake one night and, on the way from the shower to his bed, he lost his balance and fell into a bed in which another man was sleeping. The fellow came up swinging. I wasn't able to pull them apart, so I had to get over to the intercom to get help. We finally separated them."

Men who are slightly intoxicated seldom cause problems. We insist that they shower like everyone else. Most shower quickly, crash into bed, and sleep soundly for the night.

When serious abuses occur (such as men fighting, indulging in drugs, or smoking in bed), we close down the Inn for a night or two. Our intention is to bring peer pressure on flagrant violators of good order. No one likes the person who makes it impossible for others to have a place to sleep. A reasonable level of discipline is necessary. We insist that the men understand that we mean what we say. Temporary closings of the Inn get this message across to them. Word gets out fast among street people.

Rehabilitation

Regarding the chances for permanent rehabilitation of street persons, Ozanam's co-director Clem once said: "Substance abuse is rampant among street people. Almost every man who comes to Ozanam is on bad terms with his family. A very few, particularly fathers of young children, are interested in getting back together with their families. And, of course, they are deeply in need of loving support.

"It is extremely rare that a person staying at Ozanam is without a serious problem. Many say that they want jobs; however, very few actually engage in methodical searches for employment such as by using classified ads. And then, on obtaining work, few persist in their jobs. With time on their hands and money in their pockets, many go back to drinking again, especially on weekends. If only they had special interests or hobbies to occupy their minds! Or if only they could become fascinated with constructive things such as art, or gardening, or anything else that might resurrect in them an inner glow of anticipation toward good.

"Alcoholics typically have trouble with relationships. When they get angry or disappointed—as all normal people do—they easily withdraw and return to drinking. Unable to confront others in order to express their anger and disappointment so as to bring about change, they often act out their feelings inappropriately or seek consolation in alcohol.

"Here in New Orleans we have sent individuals to a local substance abuse clinic for several months of counseling in preparation for their admittance to a large state-operated rehab facility in Mandeville, Louisiana, where they reside for three to six months. Experience has shown us, however, that the majority of people who have gone through Mandeville eventually return to active alcoholism, especially if they are unwilling to make use of a support group such as AA. Inevitable disagreements arise when they return to their families. Faced with constraints, and remembering the independence they once experienced on the streets, many end up returning to the streets.

"No outside agent can change the alcoholic," Clem insisted. "The desire to change must originate from within the person. Also, there is no permanence in rehabilitation without the alcoholic recognizing a higher power from which help must be drawn."

I was curious to learn more about permanence in rehabilitation, so I asked an administrator named Joseph for his opinion.

"It's unusual for a drug addict to achieve permanent rehabilitation," Joseph said, "but sometimes it does happen. Back in 1983 one of our reformed alcoholic crewmen obtained a GS-1 government job at $13,000 a year, mapping underwater terrain. It was nothing on which he could ever get rich—but it certainly represented a chance for him to earn a steady income.

"Also, we had an unusual opportunity recently when the owner of a large apartment complex offered six of our crewmen a small apartment where they could live without paying rent. In return, they had to perform weekend maintenance on the complex. They were free to work elsewhere during the weekdays."

Cases like these are rare, but nevertheless factual. You'd be surprised at how individual homeless persons sometimes manage to rise above their misfortunes.

Trying to Treat Ailments

At one point in time, five evenings a week at Ozanam Inn were being covered by nursing volunteers. Among them was Elise, a nursing supervisor from a local hospital who volunteered three hours a week. Elise described some of the medical problems street people deal with.

"Street people suffer especially from lower-leg vascular disorders, including swellings and foot ulcerations. These come about from so much walking, standing, and sleeping in upright positions. So we nurses find ourselves treating primarily foot and leg ailments at Ozanam.

"Large numbers of street persons also suffer from respiratory diseases. Many are listless from sleep deprivation. Having been assaulted one or more times, many suffer from trauma and need long-term therapy that we can't provide. We try to steer them toward Charity Hospital. Some follow our advice; others do not. Some who go there return with stories of having had to wait eight hours in order to see a doctor. This greatly discourages them from going back there.

"It is difficult to maintain contact with individual street persons. They wander so much, and very few settle in a given locality. Thus, when treating them we assume that we will never see them again. And that assumption generally turns out to be correct."

Fifty-fifty

Charley was about forty years old. Something, it seemed, was constricting his spirit, and his repeated glances in my direction suggested that he wanted to talk. As I walked over him, his smile told me he was pleased.

He related how the Ozanam staff had taken him in from the hospital where he had been diagnosed with cirrhosis of the liver. They had insisted that he lie in bed all day long except for a few brief breaks of getting up and walking around a little, just enough to maintain his strength.

"They told me at the hospital that I have somewhat less than a fifty-fifty chance. If I am really lucky and never touch another drop of alcohol again in my life, then I might live. I don't know if I can go without liquor. But I don't want to die! I'm scared—I am really, really scared over this," he said as his eyes filled with tears.

"Look, Charley, it's clear as day that you need help. Plenty of help! You're getting a lot of help here at Ozanam—a fine bed, free meals, free medicine."

I reached for his hand and we began praying together, asking the Lord to bless the hospital staff and the Ozanam staff who had taken him in. He then spoke at length about the staff at the Inn.

"The people here promised to help me get back my health. They said that in time I can become a member of the crew, but for now I must listen to them and do exactly what they tell me to do. They will keep an eye on me and tell me when I can work and when I must rest."

"That's good, Charley. That's really good!"

He fully agreed, and half an hour later I left for home. For weeks afterwards I visited him and prayed with him every time I set foot in the Inn. He gradually seemed to improve. His skin took on a better color, he had more energy, and he smiled more than before.

"Now the staff allows me to perform light work, such as sweeping my room," he joyously exclaimed several weeks later.

Two months after that he was transferred to a hospice in Albuquerque that is operated by the Brothers of the Good Shepherd, a place where he could receive better care. Before he left New Orleans, I gave Charley a blessing, assured him that I would be thinking of him and praying for him often, and bade him goodbye.

Two years went by during which I heard nothing about Charley. Then, on meeting one of the brothers from Albuquerque, I inquired about Charley. I was told that he had left the hospice where he had been living. He just disappeared one day and has not been heard from since. Whether or not he is alive today, no one seems to know.

The Mentally Ill

One night a big fellow entered a room where I was chatting with some other men. Finding an empty chair, he hobbled over to it, flopped into it, and sat silently with his head hanging down. He remained there after the others had left, then looked at me with crossed eyes and begged me to sit down beside him.

I placed a chair up close to his, sat down, and simply listened. He reached for my hand, stroked it, then pulled my entire arm tightly against his chest. Apparently unaware of his strength, he squeezed my hand very hard, even digging the fingernail of his thumb into the bony back of my hand to the point where I could hardly stand the pain. He began to weep and he pleaded for me to help him.

"I'm scared!" he moaned. "I can't sleep at night. I keep hearing voices."

"What kind of voices?" I asked.

"My grandma talks to me. She died three years ago."

"What does she say?"

"She says for me to return to my religion. I quit my religion after she died, and now she won't leave me alone."

"Well, what do you think you ought to do? Do you want to return to your religion?"

"Yes, I guess so. But it's not easy."

"Why isn't it easy?" I asked.

"Because I don't lead a good life. It's very hard to lead a good life."

"That's true. It can be difficult to lead a really good life. But do you wish that you could lead a good life?" I asked.

"Yes."

"Well, that's the first step on your way back to the Lord, isn't it?"

"Maybe so."

On listening to him further I came to realize that, in an additive process of a sort, he visualized his repetitive sins as having pushed God further and further out of his life until forgiveness was out of the question. I reminded him of the prodigal son in the biblical story and suggested that we pray together. And so we did. He calmed down and spoke normally once more.

I said to him, "If you wish, I'll tell the staff here at Ozanam to see if they can schedule you for a visit at Charity

Hospital where they can help you. Would you like me to do that?"

"I think so," he said.

"Give me your name and your bed number, and I'll pass that information along to them."

Afterwards, when Steven had been told about this case, he had much to say about such persons—the chronically mentally ill.

"They are really to be pitied, Henry. They tend to be scavengers. Typically, they wander about as if in a daze, often conversing with imaginary listeners, some from past ages. They can be nervous, their eyes moving jerkily from left to right as if to see if they are being followed. They sometimes stop and dig into litter, coming up with strange things of imagined value such as empty cigarette packages, or discarded gum wrappers. These they tuck among their belongings before ambling on.

"They are distrustful, full of fear, and don't sleep well. The less sleep they get, the more fatigued and erratic they become. They are given medication through welfare systems that assume they will take their medicines faithfully. But by the time the medicines run out, they probably consider themselves cured and almost never return for more."

"Steven," I asked, "how large a percentage of the street people do you estimate suffer from mental disorders?"

"My guess is that about one-third of street people have serious mental and emotional disorders. They and the drug users are the ones I fear the most. Unfortunately, the signs of drug use are not always apparent. The mentally ill can usually be easily spotted because of their unusual behavior patterns, or by talking with them, when it soon becomes clear that they are not operating with 'a full deck.' The drug addicts, on the other hand, are harder to spot. Having used drugs for a long time, some have become quite skilled at concealing their condition. Drug users and schizophrenics are potentially more dangerous than alcoholics."

"How should one go about relating with them? How does one relate to persons who hardly know what's going on?" I asked.

Steven answered, "One can never go wrong by showing them kindness, the language that everyone understands. Once I realize that I am encountering a person in such a condition, I begin immediately to 'back off.' It is important not to pressure them. I have always been careful to reassure them and give them space. I became aware of this while in Albuquerque where a very belligerent mentally ill fellow often stood in line for food at the refuge where I worked. He sometimes cursed the government and the president. He claimed to have been in Vietnam and complained of not receiving the monthly checks to which he said he was entitled. It did not matter to him whether anyone was listening to him. So, when he began insisting that the president ought to be shot, I did not argue. Nor did I try to persuade this man that there was anything amiss with his philosophy, for in his case this would have set him off and we might have had violence in the dining room. He was 'teetering on the brink' most of the time.

"Putting up with demented men for twenty or thirty minutes at meal time is no great problem. We can be immediately present to them and can always bear with that temporary inconvenience. But the greater problem is to put them up for ten or twelve hours at night in a dorm with forty to eighty other men. Our concern then focuses on how such persons will be able to relate to so many others. We find ourselves hoping that nothing happens to cause them to go berserk. When relating poorly with others, they themselves sometimes decide that they must leave. We always let them go.

"By far the most lamentable of street persons are these chronically mentally ill—the ones afflicted with personality disorders, schizophrenia, paranoia, bi-polar disease, phobias, and hallucinations. These need appropriate treatment, psychotherapy, and medication but often do not receive it. Many of them have nothing to do and nowhere to go."

Bed #42

In time I somehow forgot Steven's words about allowing men to leave. A year later I found myself in the middle of a high-pressure situation.

I was speaking with two men in the third-floor dorm. Suddenly, in a nearby room, pandemonium erupted. A door flew open. Out stormed an angry, cursing man. He walked past me and came to a halt four or five paces beyond where I stood. With a fiery glare in his eyes he addressed me loudly: "I'm getting out of this damned place! Those bastards in that room are trying to cheat me in my card game! I want OUT of this damn place!"

Remaining some distance from him, I tried to calm him with words. I suggested that he try to let go of that bad experience. "After all," I said, "You have already checked into this place. Your luggage is stored away in the check-in room. You have a comfortable bed right over there waiting for you. How about letting go of that incident, staying here, and getting some rest?"

Had I been addressing a rational man, it would have been the correct thing to say. This man, however, had deep and dangerous problems. When he heard my words, his jaw tightened and he turned furiously to me. At the same time he moved his hand toward his pocket, looking as if he were about to reach for something in it.

"Look here!" he insisted. "I want nobody making fun of me! I was in Vietnam! I know how to take care of myself! And I'm ready to take care of you, too, if you don't leave me alone!"

"Sir, it's okay for you stay or to leave. Nobody here is going to give you any trouble. Nobody will try to stop you from leaving."

He slowly backed away and headed for his bed. I quietly left the dorm, went downstairs, and spoke to Marcellus, who was in charge when Steven was not there, about what had happened.

"I'll go and talk with him," Marcellus replied. "Tell me how I can recognize him."

"He's the tall, muscular white fellow wearing dark blue pajamas," I said. "When I last saw him he was standing near bed #42."

Within minutes Marcellus returned. Having told the man that he could leave, he brought him down to the first-floor luggage room, unlocked the door, gave the man his belongings, and accompanied him to the front door.

"Henry, you must never try to talk a man into staying at Ozanam if he says that he wants to leave." Marcellus's tone with me was very kind as he continued. "You never know what's on their minds. There are all kinds of people in this building, and all kinds of reasons why they might want to leave. You can, if you wish, tell them that once they leave they cannot return on that particular night."

"Don't worry, Marcellus," I said. "I've learned my lesson. It was a hard one, but you'll never find me making that mistake again!"

The Missing Ciborium

An incident occurred in 1982 that greatly disturbed the staff at Ozanam Inn. A ciborium, a goblet-like vessel containing consecrated hosts, was stolen from the tabernacle in the chapel. Left over from the Mass at which they had been consecrated, the hosts were placed in the ciborium, which was then locked in the tabernacle by the priest. Catholics believe that the consecrated hosts are the real presence of Christ, who is God.

It appeared that the sacristan had been careless with the tabernacle key, returning it to the place where it was stored for safekeeping without realizing that other people were around. One of the street men must have seen where the sacristan had put the key. During the night the man went downstairs, entered the chapel, found the key, and opened the tabernacle. He apparently took the ciborium with its hosts and consumed some wine that had been stored in a nearby closet. Empty altar wine bottles were later found nearby.

The next morning, the staff at the Inn ordered a complete shakedown in an attempt to find the missing ciborium and hosts, yet the search was unsuccessful.

Several weeks later a crewman at work found the ciborium wedged into an opening in an upstairs wall. The thief, it appeared, had been frightened of being caught with the ciborium, so he had hidden the precious object by placing it into a hole in the paneling of the wall near the showers. While later replacing the defective panel, the workman spotted the ciborium. A thorough search for the hosts was conducted, but to no avail. Sadly, the consecrated hosts were never found. The chapel was thenceforth locked at night.

Early Retirement

My co-worker Ron related to me the following story of how one family coped with a drug-addicted relative.

"I met this fellow of about thirty who seemed somewhat schizophrenic. His speech and motions were nervous and jumpy. He told of having been rejected by his family ten years earlier. His people were apparently wealthy and owned a large business.

"He got into drugs as a teenager and became unmanageable at home. So his family insisted that he leave. However, they agreed to mail him a monthly cost-of-living check so that he might have a chance to stay alive and healthy. All he had to do was inform the family of his whereabouts and they would mail his checks to the designated addresses. In effect, they were retiring him for life, but always away from home!"

On hearing this story, my initial reaction was to think rather poorly of the family. But, on mulling the whole thing over, I began to see it from the family's point of view. Obviously, they could not allow themselves to shelter and support the man's drug habit. Apparently they had tried providing him with psychiatric help, with counseling, and with moral support. If this was in fact the case, and if he had still refused to cooperate, how far should they have ridden it out with him before insisting that he leave? There are no easy answers to heartbreaking situations such as this.

Tom's Biggest Problem

Chris, one of the counselors at Ozanam, told a story about someone who had spoken to him about committing suicide. This fellow—we'll call him Tom—was about twenty years old and quite handsome. He seemed to be an athletic person, and was well spoken.

On graduating from high school and seeking employment in the business world, Tom found that he was unable to get a good job. So he took a course in welding and found immediate employment.

One day a co-worker asked him, "How would you like to make $20 a day?"

"Doing what?" Tom asked.

"Doing a very simple thing. I simply want you to deliver a package to a friend of mine," the co-worker said.

"What's in the package?" Tom asked.

"Well, I can't tell you that!"

So Tom agreed to give it a try, to deliver the mystery package after work each day. This went on for a time until the co-worker asked him another question. "How would you like to bypass the man you deliver the package to? How would you like to move up to something bigger and better, and make $100 a day?"

Tom thought it over, imagining how he might then give some of his money to his parents to show them how well he was doing. Needless to say, the package contained cocaine! When he found this out, Tom decided to try it himself, and he discovered that he felt really wonderful whenever he took it. As time went on, his dependence on the drug grew. Soon he was needing more than the $100 a day he was earning. He began going into debt, and his co-worker and others pressured him for payments. He came to feel that they might kill him unless he paid them very soon.

Tom spoke to his parents and told them about what was happening. They said that unless he stopped taking drugs they would be unable to help him and would have to ask him to leave home. Hooked as he was, it was impossible for him to change. So he left home. A loving relative took him in, but later he too had to insist that Tom leave.

When Chris met Tom at Ozanam, the young man had been in trouble with the law after having committed a burglary to support his addiction. He had the look of a frightened fugitive and was at that moment trying to avoid his probation officer. Also, he was traumatized at the thought of the drug dealers finding and killing him.

"What would you advise me to do?" he asked.

Chris advised him to stay as far away as possible from his creditors at least for now, to visit his probation officer at the earliest possible moment and explain his predicament, and then to ask him for his advice.

Chris didn't see Tom after that, but later heard that he had found a job. Although Tom had spoken to Chris about suicide, Chris came to realize that Tom's biggest problem was probably not that of committing suicide. It was fear of being murdered.

Rethinking Assumptions

Demented persons will typically philosophize in illogical ways and think about things in strange ways. "It's like this!" one man proclaimed. "We are here with a purpose like the dinosaurs! The dinosaurs are our teachers! We should keep our eyes on them! They had their time on earth to do their thing! Now they are gone! Here we are in their place with our time on earth to do our thing! Some day we, too, will be gone from the earth with nobody left to bury the last man!"

One night a tall, skinny middle-aged street philosopher had this to say: "Why work? I stay alive without working!" he boasted. "I already done this for thirteen years! Nobody's going to let me die! I sleep where I can, and I come to Ozanam two times a day for food! So why work?"

For him, success meant staying out of jail and breathing until time ran out. Hearing these words, I found myself beginning to get angry until I reflected on the brokenness of the person who had spoken them.

A somewhat different variation of the same philosophy was the following, this time from a small man with dreamy eyes: "It's like this," he began. "I'm afraid of earning money. Yes, I can earn money. I know that I can because I done it many times. But the trouble with earning money is that I can't hold on to it! I always get into trouble when I have money. I spend it on drink. Always, I spend it on drink. So I stopped working for money. I manage to live here and there. I always get by. Here I am, the living proof that I can always get food to eat. I can keep clothes on my body, and I can always find places to stay when it's dark and rainy and cold outside!"

I remind myself that, among the able-bodied, only the demented can speak of their habitual idleness as normal and good. Only they can be content with perpetually seeking from others while contributing nothing in return. I ask myself whether creativity and service to others have any place at all in their lives.

Yet their apparently skewed philosophies force me to think. I have known many who own nothing beyond the clothes and shoes they wear. In terms of material possessions, they are almost like monks who take a vow of poverty. Devoid of automobile, of house, of bicycle, of radio and TV, of refrigerator, of easy chair, of microwave oven, of a bed of their own, many street persons nevertheless remain aglow with hope of "entering the kingdom." They minister to me by giving me much on which to reflect. Repeatedly, they lead me to ponder the role of personal possessions in shaping our everlasting spirits—and to rethink my assumptions of what service to others really means.

3

LENDING AN EAR

When visiting the wanderers of society, I don't go as an expert in anything. I go simply as one human being seeking to engage with other human beings.

I discover that I must not think in terms of "converting" or "changing" the people there. To do so would be to court disappointment within myself and, thus, disengagement from them. Rather, I must meet them with the goal of affirming them as I find them, and work toward keeping hope alive in them.

Strangely, I have learned something important from their clothing, or rather, the lack of it. That is, I see them mostly after they have showered, when, during the summer months, they are dressed in only their pajama bottoms. There are no status symbols, no insignias or badges connected to this simple attire: no sergeant stripes, no captain's bars, no Roman collars; no cowboy hats or boots; no gentlemen's tuxedos with ties. Mostly their human skin shows—with or without sores, cuts, scars, or tattoos.

Thus we engage one another as ordinary people, without reference to social status symbols. Not a word is uttered about college degrees, corporate positions, famous persons we might know or have known, books we've read, places we've been, or number of years we've spent working at this or that. Our conversations quickly focus on what is of deeper meaning—health, happiness, hurts, healing, feelings, aspirations, and even—on occasion—hopeful expectations about the future.

The "Popcorn Man"

A heavily bearded young white man sat next to his bed awaiting his turn to take a shower. Our eyes met, and I went over
to chat.

"Hello!" I said. "I remember you from last week. You had
just come in from Illinois. How do you like this city so far?"

"It's okay," he said. "I been to a lot of places around here
since last week."

"Where have you stayed since last I saw you?" I asked.

"In all kinds of places," he responded. A little smile
played on his lips as he said, "You know, one night I walked
into a hotel on Bourbon Street and, boy, I was really, really
tired. I discovered that someone had left a door unlocked on
a linen closet. Nobody was around, so I crawled right into the
closet and fell asleep. I slept all night. It was daylight outside
when I awoke. So I walked out of there and, again, nobody
saw me!"

"Well, you're lucky! You might easily have awakened and
found yourself eye-to-eye with a big old cop. Have you found
any kind of work in town?" I asked.

"Yeah, I did a little work on a ship, chipping paint and
cleaning it up. I earned about $35 and I'll be getting my check
tomorrow."

"That's good! How are you feeling? The last time I saw
you, you had insect bites all over your ankles and arms."

"Yeah, that's okay now. Look! You see this scar on my
hand? That's where I cut myself with a broken bottle once.
They operated on some ligaments here in my wrist. But I still
can't move these two fingers very well.

"Yes, I see."

"Well, I went to Charity Hospital the other day and they
told me they will work on it again so that my fingers will
move."

"That's good! It's tough to lose the use of your fingers."

"Yes. Also, I have some skin blemishes on my forehead. I've noticed that they come out when I talk bad about someone. I read in the Bible once that talking bad about people brings out blemishes on the skin. It seems every time I get really mad and talk against someone I get blemishes."

"Some people get blemishes when their nerves are upset," I said. "How do you get rid of your blemishes?"

"Well, I stop talking bad, and I eat less, and I lose weight. Sometimes I try singing. When I cut down on food I get weak, but the blemishes go away. Right now I weigh thirty pounds less than I usually do."

"How about that job of yours?" I asked. "Are you going to stay with it?"

"Well, I don't know. I know a place I can rent for $45 a week. It has a refrigerator and a stove. (This was in 1985.) I'm thinking I might like to buy some popcorn and pop it there. I could sell it on the streets. I figure I could make at least $35 a day doing that."

"That sounds like something that might work," I said. "People also like hot dogs and snow cones in the summer. We call them 'snowballs' here in New Orleans. But don't forget, you'll need a license for doing that."

"Yeah. That'll cost seven dollars," he said.

"There's one thing you must keep in mind while applying for a license and selling food. People want to know that their food is clean. They first look you over to see how clean you look. That means you must be clean-looking to make money as a food vendor."

"Yeah," he said while pulling out dirty clothes from beneath his mattress. "You see these white coveralls? Well, I can throw these into a washing machine and they will look white as snow! I'll clean my fingernails and look really good!"

"And you might consider wearing a white cap," I suggested. "That always looks good!"

"Yeah, that, too! I'll have to think about all of this. You know, I don't think so good. Sometimes my mind gets dim and it takes time for me to think straight again. But I keep on trying, and the Lord helps me."

"What do you think causes your mind to go dim?" I asked.

"I don't know," he responded. "Maybe it's Satan! What do you think?"

"I think it's a mistake to blame Satan for everything bad that happens to us. Maybe your mind goes dim as a result of improper eating. Or too much alcohol and not enough healthy food. Do you agree?"

"Well, I do have a drink once in awhile. But my mind goes dim even when I don't drink."

"Maybe you're sitting around too much," I said. "Maybe you need a good exercise routine like jogging a couple of miles each day to get the blood really flowing throughout your body. People who exercise daily seem to stay in better spirits than those who sit around doing nothing."

"Maybe you're right," he said. "I don't know."

"Well, I hope you find a way of making a reliable living," I said in hopes of affirming him a little. "In listening to you, I've come to feel that you're a very good man. I surely hope you make a go of it. Hope I'll see you later. Maybe you can tell me about your successes when I meet you next time!"

"Yeah! I liked talking to you," he said. "See you later!"

On leaving him, I felt that what he appreciated most was having someone who was open to him, someone with whom he could talk. Whether or not he ever got around to selling popcorn, I do not know. To what extent he afterwards succeeded, I shall probably never learn.

"Unless Someone Takes the Time..."

Jeremy was a tall, thin, stoop-shouldered man with pointed features. He had come to Ozanam with nothing but the simple tight-fitting clothes that he was wearing. When I spoke to him, he mumbled regrets about the night before when he had been drawn to a nightclub where a big "to-do" was in progress. In his loneliness he found it difficult to stay out of a place from which such amiable noises emanated. And so he went in and began "chewing the fat" with a couple of guys at the bar who offered him a couple of drinks while they laughed. Their laughter, in fact, was the last thing he remembered before he woke up sprawled out on the ground in an alley in the rain—minus his wallet, his pocket knife, his cigarettes, and his comb. It was a hard, hard lesson to learn.

"You know, sometimes I think I'm a no-good idiot!" he said. "I'm not very smart. And trouble has a way of finding me. I try to get by without working, figuring that I'm getting ahead, getting something for nothing when people give me money. And then I seldom have money because people take it away from me and I end up begging again."

I reflect on his words and realize that most street persons have very low self-esteem. I do not mean to imply that they are necessarily humble, for humility has to do with facing the truth about oneself and acting on that understanding. It is easy for unfortunates to interpret society's lack of visible concern for them as meaning that they are "not worth the time." Unless someone takes the time to address them on at least some occasions, they easily come to believe that "worthless" signifies the truth about themselves.

The Power of Just Listening

Sometimes married couples volunteer at Ozanam. These have included Randy and Martha, Richard and Marlene, Jim and Joycelyn, and Chris and Mary. One day Chris told me this story.

"I met a man in his thirties who was on the brink of despair. He was extremely upset and totally convinced that the whole world was against him. Except for occasional part-time work he was unable to find employment, principally because of his having served time in prison.

"His family had disowned him. He wanted to prove to them that he had changed and was now all right, but their minds were set against him. He told me emphatically he was 'at the end of his rope.' He insisted that the only thing for him to do was to remove himself from this world. And as he spoke he began to weep.

"I somehow sensed that the more he spoke and wept, the calmer he grew. And as he went on, it was as if he were consoling himself. By unburdening himself to me as his listener, he was at the same time experiencing consolation. So my task was to draw him into speaking more, to 'keep him going,' so to speak. In time he seemed to become less upset and started speaking in ordinary tones. Finally, as we parted, he appeared calm and quite at peace.

"As I left Ozanam Inn that night he thanked me profusely for having listened to him when his spirits were low. I saw him three months later—looking around, smiling, and speaking with people. He said his luck had changed. Things for him had become far better than they had been. I was amazed at the fact that just listening to a person could have such a powerful healing effect."

The Alaskan Family

One night a young family from Alaska showed up at the Inn. They were a man and his wife in their mid-twenties along with their one-year-old in a stroller and a twelve-day-old infant. Hanging on the stroller was a bag containing all their travel supplies.

The infant had caught a severe cold bordering on pneumonia. As I was preparing to leave for home, Joseph, the night manager, called me aside and asked if I would mind taking the family to Charity Hospital. The fact that I was driving a van helped. The five of us plus the stroller could easily fit in my vehicle.

On the way to Charity the man told of having left Alaska and how he was planning to settle in Carolina where a house and a job awaited him.

"Where was the baby born?" I asked.

"She was born in Alabama," the father answered.

It seemed they were taking a strange route, going from Alaska to Carolina by way of Louisiana. I decided not to question them about that.

He told of having been held up, of telling the robbers that he had a wife and kids but no money, and that he ought to be robbing them instead of them robbing him. The robbers backed off and left him alone. When we arrived at Charity Hospital, I helped him unload their meager belongings. His last words to me were, "Don't worry 'bout me! I'm down right now, but I'm on my way up!"

I fully believed him because he appeared strong and determined. The plan called for them to return to Ozanam for food and help with trip preparations. I had heard Joseph mention an agency that might provide them with bus tickets to Carolina. What awesome responsibilities were theirs! Poor people! The dark circles under the wife's eyes bespoke her weariness.

Surprisingly, I ran into them a week later at Ozanam.

"I've been thinking about you all week," I said. "I thought you all would be in Carolina by now. What happened at Charity last week?"

"We couldn't leave town as planned. They found that the baby had a bad lung infection and was only an hour or two away from death," he said. "So they went to work on her and managed to get the infection under control. The baby still has a cold, but she's 90 percent okay now. We're leaving for Carolina on the early morning Greyhound. We came back here to stock up on medicine and food for the trip."

Because I was running late at the time, I got distracted and forgot to bid them farewell. Clem, Ozanam's co-director, however, was taking care of their needs, so I knew they were in very good hands.

Crisis Counseling

From the viewpoint of counseling, an overriding difficulty in our work is the fact that we seldom see a client repeatedly. Thus, we are drawn into crisis counseling situations.

In listening to the needy I ask myself: Was this person molested as a child? Is he presently in contact with his family? Is he on drugs? Does he have skills that could bring him to feel good about himself? Does he communicate in some way with a higher power? Toward what does he look forward with hope? Assuming that I will never see my client again, what shall I tell him before we part?

It was emphasized in our training that a high percentage of street people do not enjoy family support. And this I have found to be true. I often suggest that they work on improving their family relationships, perhaps by writing or phoning their families and telling them they are sorry about past disagreements. The fact is that most of them truly are sorry, but they are unable to turn their lives around. In many cases their families want nothing more to do with them.

I suggest that they continue trying to communicate, especially with their children by sending them small gifts to reassure them that they are kept in mind. At least the children can know that an unseen parent "out there" loves them. I suggest that they search for ways of using their skills to help others. And I urge them to think about God on an ongoing basis throughout the day, thanking God for particular persons and things that have meant a lot to them.

Murder on His Conscience

One very cold night, a middle-aged man started talking to me at the Inn. He was handsome, clean, well-spoken, and apparently from an affluent family. Yet he was a wanderer.

He began by telling me his story. "My father was wealthy, and he was a well-known physician. He said that he loved my brother and me, and so he never required us to do anything. We never had to work. We never raked leaves, or swept floors, or washed the family car, or made our beds, or cut grass. Always, our servants and workers did these things. On finishing high school I decided I did not want to go to college, and my father did not question that decision. So I stayed home and grew bored with life.

"In search of adventure, I decided to leave and go out West. There I met some men who ran a Mafia-like operation. Everything they did sounded exciting, so I joined them. After some time, a conflict arose between their organization and a rival group. There was a shoot-out in a warehouse in which I killed two men and strangled another to death with my bare hands."

"How do you feel about this today?" I asked. "And do you think the Lord has forgiven you?"

"I feel very, very sorry about this today. God, how I wish it had never happened! I believe the Lord has forgiven me many times over," he assured me. "But I'm not sure that I have forgiven myself. I keep thinking about the families of those men I killed. How devastated they must have been. And to think that it was I who was responsible for that. You know, I completely got away with those killings. The police never even considered me a suspect. But the memories of those murders weigh heavily on me today. It's like I'm being punished, not in prison but inside of myself."

"What do you think you might do to lighten your burden?" I asked. "Do you ever ask God to help you to forgive yourself?"

"Yes, I do," he said. "I pray very often, and I tell the Lord repeatedly how very sorry I am that this happened."

"That's very good," I said. "Is there anything you can do to help the families of the men you killed?"

"I don't think so. Maybe someday I'll track them down when I inherit money. But I would want to do that in such a way that I wouldn't expose myself to going to prison."

"What are your plans for the future?"

"Well, my father is quite old now," he said. "It appears that he'll leave a sizable estate to my brother and me. I plan to take my share and do something really good with it. I have the street people in mind. Perhaps I can use my money in some way to help them," he concluded.

"That's fine," I said. "But money has a way of changing the thinking of its owners. I suggest you try hard to stay firm in your plans to help street people."

"Well, I sure intend to! Only time will tell," he finally said.

After that conversation we parted. A year later I saw him again, but only briefly, and that was a dozen or so years ago.

No Bracelet for Christmas

In mid-December I got into a conversation with a man in his mid-forties. He spoke of having come from "red-dirt country" and I could easily believe that he was telling the truth. He seemed very downcast.

"I'm really depressed," he said. "My wife and I have split, but I keep in touch with my little daughter. She's only eight. I really love her and I want to buy her a bracelet for Christmas. I have a full-time job—I'm a mechanic—but every time I get paid I blow my check on liquor. I just can't save enough money—not even ten dollars—to buy her the little bracelet I want to give her for Christmas."

As he spoke, one could see the pain in his face. I was at a loss as to how to advise him. Clearly, his daughter was the fulfillment of his dreams, the centerpiece of his life. I suggested he phone or write to her as soon as possible. I also suggested he tell his story to one of the administrators at Ozanam Inn and ask for help in withholding part of his pay. Perhaps a savings plan could be arranged with his employer so that some of his wages could be routed to a person or agency that could help him manage the money.

I never saw him again, but I hope he was able to get his little daughter that bracelet for Christmas—not just for her sake, but also for his.

The Former Gangster

Lopez was a native of California. It was an unusual night on which he was the only person to show up for my sharing session, so we had a lot of time to talk.

"I don't know what to do," he began.

"What's wrong?" I asked. "Are you trying to make a decision or something?"

"Yes. You see, I started a gang in L.A. I spent twenty years in prison, off and on, for armed robbery and pushing heroin," he explained. "Finally I got out of prison."

He went on to explain the workings of Los Angeles gangs, how they band together and fight to protect themselves and their people from the "outsiders" who hate them.

"Then I began to break the law again," he said. "I found myself getting into trouble once more, and I saw that I'd probably end up in prison again. So I decided to leave my family and go far away. That was a year ago. I stayed in Florida. And now I'm slowly heading west once more.

"You know, I'm in my forties now and I just recently discovered the Lord. My mother is an alcoholic. When we were small she insisted that we go to church, although she herself never went. So I learned a lot about the Catholic religion. I'm no longer Catholic, but I do read the Bible and I talk to the Lord all day long. I've grown wiser and I'm really sorry about the kind of life I've led."

He explained how he harbored the hope of one day returning to Los Angeles and living a good life. He went on to
say how this hope of his posed problems: "The gang I started
is still going strong," he continued. "They respect my family
and me. If I return I'll have to tell them I've changed, and they
won't like that."

"Well, it seems to me that you can't have it both ways.
What are you planning to do?" I asked.

"I'm not sure that I'm ready to look them in the eye and
wish them well while telling them that I'm no longer one of
them."

"If you feel that way, then I know for sure that you're not
ready to return to L.A.," I said. "Where are you headed at the
moment?"

"I'm making my way to San Antonio. I'm thinking of
staying there for a time and helping to teach Sunday school. I
hear they do a lot of that kind of work there."

"Do I understand you to be asking me what would I advise you to do?" I asked.

"Yes. What do you think I should do?"

"Well, I think I hear you saying many things all at once.
I hear you saying that you love the Lord, at least enough to
want to change your life and live it his way. Is that correct?"

"Yes, I want to go straight."

"I think I hear you saying also that you have doubts
about whether or not you have the strength to go straight.
And I think I hear you asking me to reassure you in some
way."

"Yes, that's right," he said.

"Well, I advise you not to return to California for now. I
advise you to write to your family—not to the gang you
founded, you understand, but to your real family—and tell
them you're okay. Tell them that you're thinking of them.
And tell them that you've changed. But don't go back! It's
clear to me that you need more time away from home, more
time to let your new roots grow deeper."

"How much time?"

"That's hard to say. But from everything you've told me, I would say at least another five years. Maybe even ten or more. And when you go back, I suggest it be for a quick visit. It's too early to return to live there permanently."

"What should I do meanwhile?"

"I think you can't go wrong by finding a job in which you work very hard while keeping in touch with someone spiritual such as your preacher who can keep encouraging you. You need plenty of time to think and pray, Lopez, plenty of time to grow in your love for the Lord. Don't be easy on yourself. Do not 'mess things up' by acting too quickly. This might be your last chance to heal your life," I concluded.

Lopez seemed appreciative of my advice. He hugged me warmly as we were parting. Whether or not he will follow the advice, only God knows.

Always Getting Sidetracked

In spite of their failings, some street persons remain highly spiritual. Longing for something lasting and significant, they try desperately to live a life of integrity and are pained by their deficiencies. Some dream of loving but find it difficult to express love.

Some years ago, a red-faced man in his mid-thirties sought me out and said he wanted to talk.

"I am an alcoholic," he began. "I just can't seem to get my act together. Physically, I'm in good shape. I'm skilled and very capable of manual labor, but somehow I can't bring myself to work consistently over long periods of time. Always I get sidetracked by booze. Usually it happens while I'm having a good time with people. Always, I go too far! And that's a terrible experience. I don't want to go through life being this kind of person. And yet I am really this kind of person," he moaned.

"You know, I see a marvelous quality in you," I responded. "You seem to love being with people."

"I don't know," he said. "It's true that I'm good at making people laugh. And when they laugh, I laugh, too. But it always seems to end up getting me in trouble!"

"What do you mean?"

"While I'm laughing I start drinking, and when I'm having a good time I don't know how to put the brakes on my drinking. I pass out, then I wake up in some out-of-the-way place with all my money gone."

"Although you are very present to your friends," I said, "I suspect that you are somehow afraid to walk away from them and be alone with your thoughts. Am I correct?"

"I guess that's true, because I definitely don't like being alone."

"Don't you ever like being alone so that you can talk just to God in your heart? Do you ever pray?" I asked him.

"Yes, I talk to God. When I wake up in the morning and before I fall asleep at night I talk to the Lord," he answered.

"How about during the day?" I continued. "Do you thank the Lord for the light of day, for the fresh air, for the green trees, and for your health?"

"You know, I can tell that you come from a background of love," he said. "I don't come from that kind of background. I grew up in foster homes where nobody seemed to really care about me, and I spent more than a dozen years behind bars. I just can't love things and people or even myself in the way that you seem to be able to."

"You're right about my background," I said. "I did in fact come from a home where there was plenty of love. Do you have any children?"

"Well, I've had three wives and I made all three of them miserable. I also have three children."

"Do you keep in contact with your children?" I asked.

"Not really. I have a son I'm fond of. But I don't want to contact him because it will mess up his thinking to have me on his mind. Nobody can understand me. I was in prison when my boy was born. I visited him afterwards when he was one year old and I had absolutely no feeling toward him! He was like someone else's kid—like any kid on the block. Only later did I grow fond of him when he played football and I saw him do some things that I don't think I could ever have done."

"Well, at least you can take a certain pride in the fact that you brought him into this world and he is doing well, can't you?" I asked.

"I guess so. But I feel that he just 'happened' into my life, and that's the way I feel about a lot of things in my life. You seem to think of things as having come from God. I don't think that way. I don't think in terms of having received things from someone who loves me. I guess I do believe in God—after all, I did tell you I talk to him—but I'm not sure what that means."

I spoke to this man at length. We discussed people in general and how everyone continually searches for meaning in this world. He wanted to know more about God, so I started by explaining that God is the Infinite Spirit and the world is the outer expression of God's inner life; that God is in many ways like a little child who gets into everything; that God is Truth and Love and Beauty and Goodness and knows everything about each one of us; that whenever we chase after truth and love, it is God for whom we are searching in things and people and situations.

"Do you understand anything of what I am saying?" I asked.

"I really don't know," he said. "What you say sounds like it might really be true." He was silent for a minute, and then he said, "I wish that I could believe it the way you seem to believe it."

The man's problem was so deep that he may never become a normal, loving person. However, he did care enough about love and truth to confess the truth of his lack of love. And that, indeed, was a positive beginning.

Hearing Jesus Speak

Quietly I sat beside an admitted drug addict in the dormitory one evening. As we spoke, another man ambled up and joined us. The conversation turned toward religion, and the addict related his strange story.

"I was desperate for money one night, so I decided to rob a store. I was real nervous and jumpy about it. On my way there I happened to pass this church. I don't know what came over me, but I suddenly decided to go into the church. I walked in slowly, and I spotted a large crucifix up ahead. I walked up to it and began to talk to it. I was almost out of my mind.

"'Please help me, or my family will starve!' I said to the crucifix.

"You probably won't believe this, but the crucifix spoke back to me. 'I can't help you,' it said to me. 'My Father has allowed me to be nailed up here. You'll have to help yourself for me,' it said. The crucifix actually told me that!"

"You must have been surprised," I replied. "What did you do after hearing this voice?"

"I went to a bar and sold my gun to one of the customers there. Then I went out and found myself work, a lot of little jobs that kept me going."

Stories such as this one are often related by the people of the streets. A man once swore that he had personally seen Jesus Christ some years before. He said that one day when he was very sick he looked up and saw Jesus standing near the foot of his bed. Jesus reassured him that he would recover—and he did in fact recover.

Non-professional that I am, I have found myself wondering in what manner people see Jesus or hear him speak. I have asked myself whether or not it is proper for me to make any kind of judgment about that phenomenon, to consider whether or not these people were sober or intoxicated at the time of the apparitions, to try to analyze their psychological condition. What I have come to realize over time is that that the important thing is that they harbor the conviction that they heard or saw Jesus addressing them personally. They obviously treasure such memories enough to speak about them with wonder. And that in itself is very good.

Beneath the Overpass

Cecil was a twenty-three-year-old man from the Midwest. He had a beard and long hair and wore a headband. A chain hung around his neck. Unlike many street persons, he looked me straight in the eye when speaking.

"I came to find a job in this city," he said, "but I'm not having any luck."

"What kind of work do you do?"

"I used to work on a boat. Maybe I can find work on a boat here."

"I'm sure you must find it hard to be without work," I commented.

"It's rough! Sometimes I run out of money and have no food. I start to feel weak. And when I feel that way I don't have the energy to look for work."

"Do you ever have to beg for food?" I asked.

"Yes, but I don't like doing that. I sometimes drink away my money and land in jail. I just spent a month in jail in a town north of here. Afterwards, I went to my brother's house. I stayed with him for a month but I didn't get along with his wife, so I had to leave. I hitchhiked to New Orleans."

"Where did you sleep last night?" I asked.

"Under the overpass where the Interstate passes near a town called Gonzales. It was raining hard, and I made it to the overpass just in time. I was pretty dry there, but the mosquitoes ate me up. Look at my ankles and hands."

"Gosh, it looks like measles! Maybe we can put some antiseptic on it," I suggested.

"No, that's okay! The bites don't itch any more. I don't feel a thing."

"Well, at least you won't be bitten by mosquitoes here at Ozanam tonight. What was it like to be in jail?" I asked.

"It's horrible to be in jail! You get beaten by criminals. They're mad about being there, and they punch you and make you do whatever they want. I was so disgusted I hardly knew what to do."

He went on to describe the food as being awful and said that eating it was like eating grass. I asked whether the wardens protected people from abuse.

"Oh, the wardens look the other way! They figure it's part of the punishment you deserve. If I or my relatives had had money to give them, they probably would've protected me. Now that I'm out of prison, I'm finding it hard to get started again. I'm so messed up."

"Do you have a trade? Something you can do really well?"

"I'm an interior decorator," he replied.

"That takes a lot of skill. Why not study that further, get to be really good at it, and go to work for some firm as their decorator?" I suggested.

"Maybe I could do that. But if I find a job here, I'll save $90, get on a bus to New York, get me a job on a boat, and go to see a friend of mine in Europe."

"And what will you do after you see your friend?"

"Well, he really likes me, and I figure he would get me a job. Maybe he would let me stay with him."

"Suppose he can't find you a job? What will you do then?"

"Well, I won't be any worse off than I am right now," he insisted.

I reminded him that New Orleans has a large port. "You mentioned finding work on a boat here. Maybe you could find a boat that's headed for Europe."

He abruptly changed the subject. "I have a headache," he said. "Do you have any aspirin?"

"I'll go downstairs and see if I can find some for you."

I returned with the aspirin bottle, unscrewed the cap, and shook out two aspirins. Five other hands immediately shot out. Apparently not only Cecil but everyone else around him seemed to be in need of aspirins.

"I Know That Man"

How does one initiate conversations with street persons, especially if one is of quiet temperament, as I happen to be? Surprisingly, it sometimes happens in unexpected ways and in odd places, such as in the following example.

A young African-American man, about twenty years old, was sitting on the window sill in the bathroom, his back leaning lightly against the screen. He was clad only in pajama bottoms and, except for the strange look in his eyes, he was the picture of health.

He spoke constantly and in a loud voice, as if addressing a roomful of hearing-impaired people. Unlike the four other men who were sitting there smoking and quietly staring at the floor, this impetuous fellow looked around and commented on anything and everything in his line of sight. Some ten or fifteen paces away from him I stood wearing something that caught his eye.

"Hey, you!" he addressed me abruptly. "Come here, boy!" he commanded. "Let me talk to you! What you got there hanging 'round your neck?"

"This is a crucifix," I said.

"Yeah, I know—I know that man hanging on it! He's the man who keeps me going! Can I wear it for a while?"

Removing the crucifix from around my neck, I handed it to him and said, "Go ahead. I'd like to see it on you."

He placed it around his neck, adjusted it a little, and continued. "Man, I'm going to need him badly real soon because I'm about to hitchhike to Los Angeles and find me a real job.

It's been rough around here. I've been getting into trouble and I want to leave this town as soon as I can!"

"What do you do when you're in trouble? How do you keep going?"

Pointing to the crucifix, he said, "Sometimes I ask this man to keep me going and he always does. He tells me to use my mind. You know, the human mind is strong. You can change your whole life if you really want to."

"You're right," I answered. "But the mind alone is not enough. I think that something more is needed, a help that comes from outside ourselves. I don't find it so easy to change *my* life, and I think most people would agree that change is hard."

"True, that's true." he answered. "See this cigarette? I can stop smoking any time I want! But, yeah, I do need that man to help me, especially when I get around bad people. Sometimes I turn my mind away from them and just walk away. Man, you know, there's some really mean people out there. Look at these scars"—and he pointed to three on his chest. "That's where I got stabbed! I had no business being with those people."

"Have you always been good to other people?" I asked him.

"Most of the time—but not always," he responded. "I once stabbed a fellow and beat him up bad. Then I left him there and walked away. But that was wrong. That was really wrong. That's not the way I want to be! I am never going to do that kind of thing again!"

"You say that you need that man on the cross. Do you ever talk to him?" I asked. "You know, he, too, was beaten up and stabbed, and he never did anybody wrong. Do you ever pray?"

"Yeah! Sometimes—but not often. Most of the time I just don't feel like praying."

"If you don't feel like praying, why don't you tell him that?" I asked. "Why don't you tell God you don't feel like talking to him? If you speak to him like that, then you're already praying, aren't you?"

"Yeah! I guess so," he said. Then he added, "I never really thought of it that way."

"Well, I like to talk to him during the day, starting when I get up in the morning," I said. "Also, when I see a pretty sky, or when I hear good music or drink cool water, I feel that he is my special friend for giving me all of these things."

"True, that's true. I see what you mean. Where do you live, and what do you do?" he asked.

"Well, I teach here in New Orleans. And I come here one evening a week in order to help."

"Oh, I see," he said.

"Are your parents living? Do you stay in contact with them?" I inquired.

"Yeah, I see them sometimes. My mother gets mad at me for smoking pot."

"That's because she loves you. Isn't that correct?"

"Yeah, I guess so. But pot doesn't bother me," he said.

"Are you sure? Doctors are saying that pot slowly causes brain damage if somebody smokes it often."

"Well, I haven't smoked it in three days! Pot hasn't damaged my brain—I can still think good. And I can stop any time I want!"

"I wouldn't be too sure about that. Maybe you do have a good mind. But it might be even better if you'd never touched the stuff," I suggested. "Maybe it's creeping up on you, hurting your mind slowly, so that you're unable to know that it's hurting your mind."

"I never thought of that," he said. "Maybe you're right. But I never take heavy drugs. Not since I been out of jail!"

"What's it like to be in jail?"

"It's hell! I don't ever want to go there again!"

"What do you want to do with the rest of your life?" I asked.

"I want a 'sturdy' job. I want to settle down and have a little place to live. I don't want to be rich. Those rich bastards don't give a damn about people like me! They hit it lucky and keep it all for themselves. I gotta go begging them for a job!"

"There's a lot of truth in what you're saying," I responded. "However, I do know some wealthy people who seem to be very generous. I also know some not-so-rich persons who are willing to work, and they seem to get ahead. People who take short cuts often get into trouble."

"Yeah, I guess so," he concluded.

On and on we spoke for about forty minutes, during which time several other men entered the room, drew near to listen, lingered awhile, then ambled off to bed. Some seemed to nod in agreement with what we were saying. Rarely did anyone else speak. One man, also wearing only pajama bottoms, sat cross-ways on the toilet, using the open seat simply as a chair while listening to the young man and me.

Finally, we stood up and prepared to part. We shook hands and the young man left. A minute later he returned and shook my hand again. We agreed that we would think of each other often and remember in a very special way the night that we talked.

I left Ozanam that evening profoundly impressed by this young man's openness, and by the fact that he had publicly confessed to serious wrongdoing. How repentant he was! More contrite, I think, than many self-righteous persons I have known. The impact of the conversation lingered in my mind throughout the following day. I found it easier to wonder at it than to evaluate it.

4

"THE LORD GOD MADE THEM ALL"

People from all walks of life come to Ozanam Inn. Discovering who they are can be both surprising and painful.

I have in mind a tall, thin man, a fellow with the heavy odor of alcohol on his breath. He approached the front door of the Inn and, even though Ozanam refuses to take in heavily intoxicated persons, Brother Matteo decided to make an exception for him, because it was bitterly cold outside and the fellow was clearly under-dressed. Besides, he was able to navigate without assistance, although barely so.

On seeing him, what immediately caught my eye was the large rectangular Johnson & Johnson bandage dangling from his forehead. Someone must have struck him a blow, perhaps a week earlier, for the blood on the bandage seemed dark and dry. Except for a solitary strand of tape, the adhesive was no longer effective. Thus, the bandage swung back and forth like a pendulum across his left eye and cheekbone as he swayed up the front steps. It bothered me that no one had taken the trouble to remove that useless mess of a first-aid dressing.

Half an hour later I saw him minus the bandage. Quietly, I entered the office where he was sitting stoop-shouldered on a sofa, his shirt collar pulled up high to his ears. Several minutes went by. He turned slowly to look in my direction and then asked my name.

"I'm Deacon Henry," I responded.

"Do you have anything to eat, Henry?" he asked. "I haven't eaten in two days."

"Well, it's pretty late and the kitchen is probably closed. But I'll go and see if I can find someone who might let me in. Maybe I can scrounge up something for you."

Feeding the hungry outside of scheduled times, I once discovered, is not as simple as it sounds, even at Ozanam. The moment one brings food into a room where there is a hungry man, others in the room immediately declare themselves to be starving. I somehow managed to maneuver my man into a different room, out of sight of the others. There he sat until I finally brought him food from a donor's box.

"Well, here's something for you! It's not exactly what you would order at Arnaud's Restaurant. It's only three sweet rolls, but they will at least put something in your stomach to tide you over 'til breakfast!"

He seemed very appreciative. As he reached for the rolls, I could see his handsome features beneath his long, shaggy hair and lengthy growth of beard. I judged him to be highly gifted, as he spoke in flawless English, occasionally using a classical phrase or two that I, myself, would hesitate to use. I waited for the food to begin settling in his stomach.

"Where are you from?" I asked.

"California," he responded. "I was an actor."

"What are you doing here in New Orleans?" I asked.

"Well, things didn't work out in California the way I expected them to," he said.

It was a sad story, one I had heard many times from those who drop out of the mainstream of life.

"I notice from your speech that you must have had a good education," I noted.

"Yes, I did," he replied. "I studied speech and drama at Xavier University. Afterwards I went to California and did quite well for a time. Then things began to change. My wife and I got caught up in a swirl of social activities and glamorous living. We began attending parties. Too many parties. Invitation after invitation came our way and we hated to turn them down because we met important people at the socials."

The lengthy silences between his remarks told me that he was not anxious to speak any further. So I left him alone. He was exhausted, barely able to make his way up the stairs to the dorm. When last I saw him he was easing himself into bed, allowing the pull of gravity itself to do most of the work. Like so many in his pitiful condition, he wanted merely to sleep.

For tonight, at least, he would have a warm, dry bed, food in his stomach, and shelter from the cold and rain.

The Innocent and the Helpless

Numbered among the street people are the educated, the kind-hearted, the ignorant, the cruel, and, of course, the con artists and the criminally psychotic. Undoubtedly, numerous such persons are sheltered among the innocent and the helpless at Ozanam Inn as at any shelter that takes people in off the streets.

Although Ozanam's facilities allow for the lodging only of men, women occasionally knock at the door. Such was the case with Sarah, an African-American lady of about thirty who came to the front door for a sandwich after dark. Her left arm was heavily bandaged. As she was standing at the door, she saw a man coming up the walk behind her and she reacted with total panic. Pushing her way forward, she whispered nervously to David, who was manning the door that night, "David! David! Look—right behind me! That's the man who tried to rape me last week!"

David immediately led the woman into the house and brought her into a side room where I happened to be sitting. Then he called the police. While awaiting their arrival, Sarah agitatedly told me her story.

"Did you see that man a few feet behind me?" she asked.

"No, I didn't."

"That man out there! He's the one who pulled a knife on me last week! It was getting dark, and I was in a building not far from here. He came up behind me in the hallway. He pointed at a door and said, 'You get into that room!' So I jumped through a window and got all cut up. I crashed down on the street and broke my arm and called for help. They called an ambulance."

"Gosh, that's awful!" I said.

The arrival of two patrolmen interrupted our conversation. They quickly got a description of the man Sarah had seen. Naturally, he had fled.

The incident ended with David sending Sarah to her apartment not far away under the escort of three trusted men from the crew at Ozanam. I heard nothing further about this case, but the image of this frightened woman has remained in my memory and she has remained in my prayers.

Retiring His Gun

Catholics often confess their sins to a priest. In working with street people, I have been amazed at how certain individuals spontaneously confess their sins to others.

Several of us were gathered one night for scripture reading. The subject of God's merciful forgiveness came up and, after a moment of silence, one of the men, a native of Alabama, said in a soft voice, "You know, I think I killed somebody once."

"Would you like to tell us about it?" I asked.

"Yes, I would." he said. "It happened when I was young. We were stupid back then. We had no sense. My friends and I were running near a supermarket. I grabbed one of the grocery carts and ran it into an old lady. I knocked her down real hard. Her head hit the bumper of a car as she fell. Nobody saw us. We then ran off."

"Are you sure she died?" I asked.

"Yeah, I read about it in the paper the next day. But, you know, that was when I was all mixed up and had no sense. I'm not like that any more."

"I also shot my brother," he continued. "We got into an argument and he told me to get out and not come back. So I shot him in the leg. He's okay now and we're friends again."

"Do you think the Lord has forgiven you for all of that?" I asked.

"Oh yes! He forgave me long ago. But some people I know haven't forgiven me. They keep telling me to hit the road, to keep away from them, and to get lost. And I do stay away from them. I don't want any more trouble."

"Have you gotten rid of the gun you used?" I asked.

"Well, not exactly," he said. "I don't carry it on me all the time, but I keep it on stand-by not far away."

"How long do you think it will take you to 'turn the corner' and put that weapon away for good?"

"I don't know. I hope it'll happen soon. But I just don't know," he said.

I saw him a month or so later and asked whether he had retired his gun.

"Not yet," he responded. "Give me a little more time," he pleaded. "It will take a little more time, but I hope to get there someday soon."

Voices from the Tomb

I met her at a hospice for the elderly, the quiet, mild-mannered lady with a "past" whom I shall call Ethel. Ethel was well into her eighties and, on learning that I was writing about the homeless, she volunteered to relate this very unusual story to me.

"My father died when I was a child, and my mother drank. So, I was placed in an orphanage. I ran away from the orphanage when I was ten and went into a freight yard. The weather was bad and I asked some boys to help me into a boxcar. They lifted me up and then went away. A little later the train took off with me in the boxcar. It traveled all night long, and the next day some people saw me in there and called the railroad office. They stopped the train, got me out, found my aunt, and had her come and get me. But I wanted to get away from her. She was kind to me, but I was a mean sort of kid and I always ran away from her.

"I met a preacher whose son raped me. I was only eleven at the time, so my aunt put me in a house for young women, and there they sterilized me. I stayed at that house until I was eighteen. When I left there, my aunt was supposed to have someone meet me at the station, but nobody showed up except a very kind lady who happened to be a prostitute. I went to her house and, in time, I myself got into that profession.

"While I was still young, some other girls and I decided to go out and live on the streets. We found a really big cardboard box—something that must have been used for a refrigerator or such—and we took it into a cemetery where we made a little house to sleep. We soon got to know what was going on in the cemetery.

"There was a story going around that every night at midnight one could hear the spirits crying out in the cemetery. Well, it wasn't true, and I know that for sure. It was a woman who was yelling in a tomb. I knew the woman personally. She and her man were sleeping there. They were living in a vault that had a loose door. He managed to pry open the door and was able to close it behind him. He was a wino, and every night he would beat her. And she would cry—that was the sound that people heard. Can you imagine? They were living together for months in that graveyard vault!

"I went to work in a beer garden and later met a World War II draft-dodger who led me into trouble with the law. I became an alcoholic and was in and out of jail for years. On getting out of prison I began sleeping in a park. I got hold of a blanket and a pillow and slept there in a park shelter. In the daytime I hid my things high up on a shelf inside the shelter where nobody could see them. I would go out and drink heavily and get intoxicated. But before I passed out I always managed to find my way back to my shelter in the park. I'd reach up to get my blanket and pillow, and then I'd lie down and sleep it off until morning. Being a woman, I was often pestered by men, but I was never raped or robbed, at least not in those days. I loved nature, and that's why the park appealed to me so much.

"Somehow I learned to forgive all the people who did me wrong. I was no angel myself. I was a 'bitchy' kid, and I guess I got what I deserved. But I am happy today. I have a good place to stay and good food to eat, and I know many people who are very kind to me. Look at Jesus! He forgave people, so I forgive them, too."

The Reverend Cons

One night at Ozanam we took in two two men who had convinced the brother on duty that they were priests. One of them wore the long black cassock that was used by priests in those days.

Feeling that it would be inappropriate to have the priests sleep in the dormitory, the brother in charge put them up for the night in two of the six bedrooms we had in our brothers' living quarters. They joined us at the evening meal. The older man claimed to be a priest in one of the Eastern rites in union with Rome. The younger fellow, a black man in his twenties, claimed to have been assigned as assistant pastor to nearby St. Patrick's Catholic Church. He said he had reported there that evening but that nobody had been there to let him in, and so he had come to Ozanam to spend the night before reporting again to St. Patrick's in the morning. Neither of their stories sounded right to me. So, as we ate dinner, I began to ask a few questions.

The elder man claimed to have a brother in Florida who was a bishop. He asked us for air fare to that state and assured us that his brother would refund us for the ticket. I asked more questions, such as about the seminary he had attended, and so forth. Finally, I asked him to lead us in our evening prayers. He firmly declined.

Privately I told my associates that I suspected neither of the two was a priest. Then, an hour later, we met the pastor of St. Patrick's at a funeral wake.

"Guess what, Father!" I exclaimed. Your new assistant pastor is spending the night with us at Ozanam!"

He looked at me with a twinkle in his eye.

"Is he a young black fellow wearing a cassock?" he asked.

"Yes, he is."

"He was at my door this afternoon," the priest continued. "He told my secretary that the archbishop had sent him to us as our new assistant pastor."

The pastor had ended up turning him away, threatening to call the police if ever he returned, for nobody is ever assigned to a parish as an assistant pastor without the pastor knowing about it well in advance. The other fellow—the one who had claimed to be a priest in one of the Eastern rites in union with Rome and said he had a brother who was a bishop—told us he was a good friend of one of the brothers assigned to Camillus House Refuge in Miami. He had given us the correct name of the brother—Paul. After he retired to his room, I phoned Brother Paul in Miami.

"Brother," I said, "We have with us tonight a man who claims to be a good friend of yours. He says his name is Father George."

Brother Paul started to laugh.

"George," he said, "is indeed a friend of mine! He is an ordinary street person and he has been in and out of this refuge many times. I am amazed that he gave you his real name!"

The outcome was that we decided to allow the two men to stay for the night, but in the dormitory with the other street people.

Travel by Caboose

Ted was a deeply tanned, macho-looking white man of about forty. His pal, a little sleepy-eyed fellow, seemed to agree with everything he said. They told of having hitchhiked to New Orleans from Vancouver, British Columbia. But their mode of travel was unlike that of most hitchhikers.

"You mean to say that the two of you came all that distance by train?" I asked.

"Yep! We made it all the way on freight trains," Ted said. "It took us twenty-seven days in all. We made it mostly by caboose. Once or twice we rode up front in the locomotive."

"Seems to me that traveling that way could be dangerous," I said. "I've heard that freight train crews hate hitchhikers and sometimes treat them cruelly, even pushing them off the train while it is moving at high speeds."

"Sometimes that's true," he said. "But it's rare. I always make friends with the caboose man before climbing aboard. Most of them are lonely and want someone to talk to during their long, boring journeys. If you can get them to like you, then you have it made. We always get their permission before stepping aboard the train."

"Aren't they breaking rules by taking you aboard?" I asked.

"Maybe they are—I don't know. That's not my problem."

"Where are the two of you going from here?"

"We're thinking of going to Colorado, then maybe to Wyoming or some place like that. We like Western things like rodeos. I've done some riding myself, but now I'm getting a little too old for that rough stuff!"

Cheating the Electric Chair

While I was working at Ozanam I came to know a condemned man whom I shall call Pierson. I visited Pierson several times at the local Orleans House of Detention. One day I learned that he had been transferred to the faraway Louisiana State Penitentiary at Angola, so I afterwards corresponded with him by mail.

Pierson had killed a cashier during a robbery. Claiming that he had come from a family of alcoholic parents, he maintained that he was not deserving of death because he had been drunk at the time of the killing. He insisted that the public defender had done a very poor job, and Pierson was convinced that he did not really belong on death row.

Early in our relationship I made it clear that I would not engage in legal tactics on Pierson's behalf. My principal role would be to correspond with him regarding things of the spirit, to help keep open his lines of communication with the outside. Thus, when writing to him I sent him stamps so that he might be able to write to whomever he wished.

"I cannot imagine myself being fried like an animal in the electric chair!" he insisted. "I refuse to think that here in this country they could subject a person to such an indignity."

It happened that Pierson was an excellent cartoonist. And so, almost every letter I received from him featured a colorful cartoon on the front and rear of the envelope.

"What talent this man has!" I told my family. "I can easily picture him at work as a professional cartoonist for a widely read newspaper."

Pierson lingered on death row for at least five years, writing to me once a month and sometimes more frequently. In his letters he summed up a life in which past failures had added up to a present graveyard of defeats. He mentioned having been too busy in the past to think about life until he found himself in the shadow of death. Finally, with time on his hands on death row, he read the Bible cover to cover. He claimed that he had emerged from that experience a changed man, and wrote at length about the Lord being his shepherd, his one true hope, his everlasting friend.

He once came within three days of execution before the governor granted him a stay. Sometime later he wrote to tell me that he had come down with cancer of the lungs (he had always been a heavy smoker), and stated that he was continually under heavy guard in the prison hospital. A month later I received word that he had died.

Amazingly, it was Easter Sunday morning when the Lord took his soul! Knowing how Pierson's mind worked, I sensed that he would have felt that his death in the hospital had cheated the executioner. Somehow it seemed to me that Pierson the cartoonist had in the end scored a victory, something perhaps comparable to that of a penitent thief long ago on Calvary.

Scared

Clarence was clean and neat, and he seemed fairly well educated. He was residing temporarily at the Inn while searching for a rooming house. He had found a job and was looking forward to new beginnings. Street life was about to end for him, and he was in the mood to philosophize about it a little.

"You know, I was a street person for a time," he said. "For only a month or so until better luck came my way."

"What is it like to be a street person?"

"Actually," he said, "there are two kinds of people out there." He paused for a few seconds and then went on. "There are the street people, and there are the homeless people. Street people are the ones who prefer living on the streets. Street living has become their way of life. Some are running away from the law, from child support mandates and things like that. They've given up on ever accomplishing anything, and obligations no longer concern them. They hate being regimented in any way.

"Then you have the homeless. They're out there because of a setback. They're roaming around in hopes of finding a way of getting off the streets and settling back into regular living. That's the kind of person I was when I was living on the streets."

"How did you come to be living on the streets?"

"Well, my father and I had some big disagreements and he kicked me out. So I took to the streets. I tell you, being on the streets is really scary—especially if you're alone."

"How is it scary?"

"First of all, you have feelings of low self-worth and defeat. You are convinced that nobody cares about you and that you're like a clump of dirt or worse. It's not as bad if you find a good buddy out there, someone you can trust, and you can watch out for each other. There's a lot of danger out there, and the buddy system helps a lot!"

"Danger such as what?" I asked.

"Say that you get a room in a flop-house. You wake up in the middle of the night to go to the bathroom. But you hesitate to go because you're scared."

"Scared of what?"

"Scared that someone might hurt you! You don't know who might surprise you with a knife or a gun in the bathroom and force you back into your bedroom and work you over. They're after money for drugs, and they might get what little money you have and even kill you for it. The fear of that is just horrible! And sometimes, because of that fear, people choose to urinate and defecate in a bedroom rather than chancing a trip to a bathroom. It's really frightening and awful."

"Wow! I hadn't ever thought of that," I responded.

"And the same is true every time you find yourself alone in a place where you know someone could step from out of the shadows and assault you. You cannot assume that people will leave you alone," Clarence concluded.

Motorcycle Man

Tony was a short, husky man of about thirty-five, the owner of a big and powerful motorcycle. As a member of the crew at Ozanam for some time, he had gained the confidence of many. He spoke in positive ways about the Inn and insisted

that it was a privilege to be associated with the good people
he found there.

A day came when Tony, seemingly in a spirit of generosity, mentioned that he wanted to raffle off his motorcycle for
the benefit of the Inn. And so, with permission from the Inn's
staff, he went around selling chances over a period of two or
three weeks. He himself was to conduct the final drawing for
the winning ticket on a certain well-publicized day. I purchased one of his tickets, which he was selling for a dollar
apiece, and began asking myself what I would do if I were to
win such a fancy machine. A week later he asked me to pur-
chase more tickets, but I refused.

Finally, the day of the drawing came and went. When visiting the Inn several days later, I asked who had won the raffle. Who was the proud owner of the shiny big machine?

"Well, it's like this," someone said. "In the pre-dawn
hours of the day of the drawing Tony left the dorm, apparently to go to the toilet. No one at the Inn saw him after that.
We figure he must have sneaked outside while carrying the
raffle money, pushed his motorcycle silently down the block,
started it, and took off for parts unknown! We don't expect
to see Tony or the raffle money ever again."

This incident took place some fifteen years ago and, indeed, no one has seen Tony to this day. Following his depar-
ture, speculation ran high. Weeks later people were speaking
of him as probably in some God-forsaken place—perhaps in
Albuquerque, or California. Maybe even in Wyoming. The
new ground rule was: No more raffles of anything at
Ozanam Inn!

The "Poet Laureate"

Jim was the good-looking son of a high-ranking foreign service officer who was then nearing retirement. A young man of
about thirty, he claimed to be a poet and showed me some

writings he said were his own. He seemed talented and said he was looking for a free place to live. He pictured himself as deserving of this because he felt he was worthy of the title "poet laureate" and insisted that others across the pages of history have enjoyed such privileges.

"I don't understand, Jim. You mean to say that you want to be a full-time poet without a sideline of any kind? To be a poet without also teaching English or doing something else for pay?"

"Yes! Why not?"

"Well, I don't know how good you are at poetry. Realistically speaking, are you so good at poetry that you will sustain yourself continuously in today's world on poetry alone?" I asked.

"Oh, very definitely," he responded, and went on to tell me of how he hoped to find a patron, a wealthy person who would employ him as his or her permanent poet-in-residence. He imagined his patron giving him the free use of an apartment and, perhaps, even an automobile.

"Nothing elaborate," he would say. "Maybe the kind of apartment owned by well-off people, like an apartment over a backyard garage."

He imagined his living quarters as being in a truly idyllic place, a beautiful setting tucked among oaks or palms with a picturesque little stream nearby. He pictured his patron providing him with meals and a living allowance, and insisted that his goal was not to become wealthy, but only to write poetry. There, in his imagined apartment, he would live and work, spending all his hours writing wonderful poetry until his dying day.

Unrealistic dreams die hard in the streets, and so I told Jim that, realistically speaking, I thought the chances for his dream coming true were very slim. He was a temperamental young man who quickly dismissed my opinions with a frown. I made it clear that I hoped that time would prove me wrong, and I wished him the best as he moved forward in search of

greener pastures. I never saw Jim again, and I wonder to this
day if, perhaps, I may have been a bit too hard on him.

"I'm Not Angry"

Theologians tell us that, being the fullness of perfection, God
is unchangeable. Thus, I am often amazed over the ways in
which people visualize God as becoming more angry, or less
angry, at people. For example, the writer of Isaiah 12, states:
"I give you thanks, O Lord; though you have been angry with
me, your anger has abated, and you have consoled me."

At Ozanam Inn I met Eric, a man familiar with biblical
passages like this one. He told of having lived in buildings of
varying degrees of shabbiness, buildings inhabited by rats,
roaches, and other creepy-crawlers. Eric drifted across the nation and ended up in the settlement of Venice at the mouth of
the Mississippi, where a deputy convinced him that better op-
portunities awaited him elsewhere. He had then come to
Mardi Gras City, where he had recently received a beating
from a huge man who had demanded his money. The black-
ness around Eric's eyes and the scratches across his face and
forehead confirmed his story. Inasmuch as we were speaking
in the context of religion, I asked Eric, "Do you think that you
can forgive that man who did these very cruel things to you?"

"I'm not angry at him. Really, I'm not angry. Not in the
least!" he insisted. "I can't forgive him because I don't hold
anything against him. The Bible says that we must never
judge others. Only God is able to judge. So, you see, I'm not
angry at him."

"That's fine." I said. "When we continue to hold anger
within ourselves, we end up feeling the urge to kill. After having been hurt by another, we easily end up increasing our own
hurt. We should strive never to store up anger."

"That's absolutely right," he responded. "Only God can
judge that man who beat me."

He paused a moment in deep thought, and then he continued. "I'm not angry. But when I think about it, I realize that God must be very, very angry with that man—because that bastard really did me wrong!"

The Student from Cape Cod

During the mid-1980s I was frequently amazed by the number of men who came from faraway places in search of work in economically depressed Louisiana. One man in particular stands out in my memory—a handsome, alert, and well-spoken young fellow of about twenty. Because of his excellent vocabulary and clear articulation he immediately stood out. He was deliberate, outspoken, and very direct with people, obviously full of self-assurance. I liked him immediately, but I also understood that, at that time, a vast segment of the male population of my native state would probably dislike him, for he was an educated African American from the North.

"Hi!" I said. "I remember that when I registered you downstairs you said that you come from Massachusetts. You're kind of far from home, aren't you? What do you think of our hot, humid weather down here?"

"Yes, it's burning hot down here. I come from Cape Cod where there's always a breeze, and I miss it."

"You told me that you are enrolled in a college near Boston. What do you study?"

"I'm halfway through college at present," he replied. "My major is physical ed. I came down here for the adventure of finding a summer job. I usually work on a six-hundred-passenger boat operating off the coast of Cape Cod. A skipper there told me about the fleet of boats used to service offshore oil rigs in Louisiana, especially around Oil Town [not its real name]. So I flew to New Orleans and took a bus out to Oil Town. And, boy, did I learn a lot!"

"What do you mean?"

"Well, I spent a week in Oil Town looking for work. I was more than qualified for the simple jobs they listed for work on boats. But always I seemed to get the runaround. I'm sure it's because I'm black. I could think and speak better than almost every person I contacted. And yet they strung me along!"

"You do speak very well," I said. "Your diction is excellent, and you seem to be very bright."

"Some of those men were shallow and I could see right through them and the excuses they gave. What they told me by their actions was, 'I don't want any smart blacks on my boat if I can help it, but I'm not going to come right out and tell you that!' They don't realize how stupid they seem."

"I agree with you," I replied. "Years ago I worked around Oil Town myself, and I know what you mean."

"I see them driving big cars," he continued. "They look so successful and satisfied with themselves, but you ought to hear how stupid they sound when they speak. They call it Cajun talk! And the way Oil Town is run—it's insane! That place is dripping with oil money, but civic projects are almost totally neglected. There's no recreation program or center for young people. And what they call their library is a laugh! The place looks unbelievably shabby. Why do people live like that when there's so much money around?"

"I often ask myself the same question," I replied. "Many of them seem to be most comfortable with a sloppy home and a sloppy appearance. Some were poor until recently. I don't think that they can be expected to change overnight."

"Well, I could tell them how best to use their money if they would listen to me," he said.

"What would you say to them if you had the chance?"

"I would tell them to use their wealth to educate themselves and open up their stupid closed minds!"

"When you speak that way, you're including about 90 percent of the human race, aren't you?"

"Yes, I am," he said. "Why don't people 'wake up and smell the coffee'?"

"I don't think it's that simple," I replied. "Uneducated people need someone to inspire them. Otherwise they get high-paying jobs such as on oil rigs and blow their money on worthless stuff. It takes time for them to understand that things like money, fine cars, and beautiful homes don't make us into better persons. What are you planning to do now that you've decided you don't like Oil Town?" I asked.

"Well, I'm going to call home and ask them to wire me some money. Then I'll go to Florida where I have friends and see if there's anything good to be found on boats there. If things don't work out for me in Florida, I can get on a plane and be home in less than one day. It's no sweat. I'm having an adventure. Maybe I'll even go to the West Coast. I'll just play it by ear."

"You are very fortunate! Look at the other men in this dorm. Like you, most of them have no job. But, unlike you, most of them suffer from alcoholism or other addictions. And their families, too, are suffering. Unlike you, most of them cannot wire home to get air fare."

"Yes, I guess I really am lucky! That's correct—I really am very lucky," he repeated as we parted.

The End of the World

Understandably, a vast number of those in the street community believe that the end of the world is near. Wishing to know more about this one night, I asked several questions following a man's assertion that the end is certainly upon us.

"Do you think the world will end before next week?" I asked.

"No, not really." he answered.

"How about next month? Do you think you and all of us here at Ozanam will be alive on earth a month from now?"

"Yes, I guess Ozanam will still be here. I sure hope so!"

This particular conversation took place in 1985. I contin-

ued by asking, "Do you think the world will end before the
year 2000? Or do you think we should stop investing in the
future and simply wait for the end to arrive because it's so
very near that we can't really get started on anything new
since there's no hope of completing it?"

"No, I don't think so," he finally admitted. "I guess most
of us here will see the year 2000."

It was not long before this progression of questions had
led several of the others present to admit that the end might
not be as near as they had at first imagined. Somehow, the
translations of fantasies into definite time periods evoked a
somewhat different response from them.

Before leaving the subject of doomsday, I made it clear to
the man that in questioning him the way I did, I was not
maintaining that the world would definitely not end very
soon. For, indeed, we were not on the best of terms with the
Soviet Union at the time. I went on to explain that it is not
given to us to know the day or the hour, and pointed out that
the end of our life on earth is, in fact, a kind of end-of-the-
world for us, at least in our personal experience of this world.

Not Supposed to Get Caught

In the presence of a dozen men, Willard, a thirty-or-so-year-
old man, related the painful experience of discovering his wife
visiting an old boyfriend of hers.

"It happened a year or so ago when we were living in St.
Louis," he began. "Someone told me about what she was
doing. So, I followed her at a distance as she went to meet
that dude. When she came back home I asked her where she'd
been. She lied and lied about it. But I seen her with my own
eyes! I seen her enter his apartment next to a filling station. I
was really mad, so I beat her with a big ruler—a yard stick."

"How do you feel about that incident today?" I asked in
the presence of the other men.

"Well, I can't tell you how much she really, really hurt me," he said. "I was terribly upset and grieved that she would do a thing like that to me."

"Do you think it was right for you to beat her as you did?" I asked.

"No, it wasn't right. I know that I did wrong by beating her. But you know what hurt me even more than that?

"What?"

"Well, I told the whole story to my mother-in-law in the presence of my wife. You would never believe what she said. She looked at her daughter and said, 'Don't you know that you're not supposed to get caught when you do things like that?' It was weird! I couldn't believe what I was hearing!"

Survival Techniques

Some street people are highly skilled and cunning in their survival techniques. I was made aware of this in 1990 when a street man related to me how another man he knew would stand at a street corner all day. Around his neck he had a sign that read: I WILL WORK FOR FOOD! Automobiles began to stop. Thinking that he was starving and also willing to work, some of the people gave him their phone numbers or business cards so he could call and arrange to work. Others simply gave him money—and some days he would collect up to $200! At the end of the day he would pocket the money and tear up all the cards and slips of paper with the phone numbers. Every day he changed locations and every day he just kept right on collecting big money.

Steven, Ozanam's director, once spoke to me about some of the strategies used by street persons. "It is interesting to observe the survival techniques used by some of them. For example, a man knocked on the door at Ozanam Inn one day. 'I need to use a bathroom badly!' he shouted. 'I'm a Catholic, and I wonder if you would allow me to use your bathroom.'

"'Come in,' I replied. 'You will find the men's room down the hall and to your right. It's a good thing you're a Catholic,' I kidded. 'Were you a Baptist or a Muslim, you know, I would refuse to let you use the toilet!'

"He caught on to my joking.

"Occasionally my friends complain of the homeless telling lies. One must remember, however, that the homeless seldom view such statements of theirs as lies. This became especially apparent one day in the case of a young man who 'hired' himself and a buddy into Ozanam Inn. He came as one of the street persons checking in for the night. Paying close attention to what was happening, he apparently learned my name and overheard someone say that I was about to depart on a trip. So, immediately after I left, he found a bucket and mop and began to work at cleaning the floors. Marcellus, who was in charge during my absence, questioned him about his appearance on the scene.

"'I'm the new man Steven hired. If you don't believe me, then ask Steven!' he said.

Marcellus had no way of checking out the story, and the fellow seemed to be a diligent worker. A little later, as Marcellus passed him in the hall, he spotted a second young man hard at work nearby. The first man told Marcellus that the second one was the other worker Steven had hired.

I returned several days later, and Marcellus asked, "'What about those two young fellows?'

"'What do you mean?' I asked.

"'They say you hired them just before you left. I'm wondering why you hadn't told me.'

"'I didn't hire anyone before I left. Those guys are pulling one over on you!' I said.

"So we confronted them. They laughed and insisted that they had harmed no one. They had worked well and contributed to the Inn. They begged us to retain them on the crew. We took a liking to them and they won us over to their point of view. We kept them on the crew and they did a credible job over the next few months while they stayed with us."

5

STORIES FROM BIBLE SHARING

In the late 1980s, the decision was made to shift our strategy somewhat for working with the homeless at Ozanam Inn. Rather than simply speaking with them individually on a "catch as catch can" basis, we would start inviting them to group gatherings. Thus began our Bible-sharing sessions.

Intended to bring the homeless a moment of hope, something on which they could build their dreams before returning to the stark realities of street life, the Bible-sharing sessions offer a chance to hear the word of God and then to respond by sharing personal experiences. At six in the evening we invite the homeless to "come as they are" and meet in the chapel. We try always to conduct the Bible-sharing sessions in the context of a Christian meeting favoring no particular denomination. That is, we choose readings that concentrate on what is held in esteem in the minds of all Christians.

The Triumphal Ones

Always, one makes oneself vulnerable when working with street people. The persons whom I've always found hardest to relate with during the sharing sessions are the self-righteous who enter the chapel with their personal leather-bound scriptures tucked beneath their arm. Turning aside from a copy of the Good News Bible I offer them, they insist on following my readings in their own personal Bible, a practice that's fine with me.

One particular fellow sat silently throughout my session. He said not a word until the meeting was about to end. I had just read the scriptural passage about Jesus saying he is the Way, the Truth, and the Life. I then proceeded to give other names by which God is known, and I explained how we can see the good, the love, the beauty, the wonder of creation and move on immediately to bless the Lord from any place we happen to be.

The man stood up and loudly criticized me for "indoctrinating the men" with what (according to him) were my own ideas. Holding his Bible above his head triumphantly, he declared all utterances of private religious understandings to be suspect.

"You have only to read from this book!" he loudly insisted while tapping the book with the palm of his other hand for emphasis. "It speaks for itself! It carries the power to defeat Satan! Whoever keeps his eyes totally on it will overcome anything that is evil in this world!" The man's parting words as he walked out of the chapel—because, as he said, he was tired after working all day—were "You ought to stick to the Bible!" Perhaps he spoke as he did because of an inner need to stand up and acclaim the word of God and thereby know himself as one who speaks out on God's behalf. Naturally, I was disappointed that he had targeted me in the process and, while doing so, had given me no chance to reply.

In spite of such setbacks, I try to let go of my disappointments, place such people in God's hands, and focus my attention on those who can be helped by my service.

Endless Levels of Understanding

As a book of hope and love, the Bible is highly revered by most street people. About one in five seem to be familiar with it to the point of being able to quote at least a passage or two from it. I am sometimes surprised by the erudite bits of understanding that some of the street people have.

Toward the end of a session one night I mentioned different names for God. "You know, we call God our Father," I said. "However, God is known by many other names. Some of those names are Love, Goodness, Truth, Beauty, Patience, Light, Presence, the Faithful One, Wonder!"

I ended with the statement, "This might be hard to understand, but God is also said to be Existence Itself. Can you imagine what that means?"

Immediately a hand went up. A man who looked about thirty years old responded, "Yeah! Doesn't that mean something like 'I will be present to you?'"

I was astounded.

"Yes it does!" I responded. "Old Testament scholars tell us that as far as they can tell the term means something like 'I will be present as I will be present.' Where did you hear this?"

"I was watching a TV show on the Bible one night and somebody said that."

Admittedly, I become too philosophical at times. But occasionally I am brought soundly down to earth by a street person.

While addressing a small group on still another night I drifted somewhat. "Try to understand," I said, "that God loves you more than you or I could ever imagine. God loves every one of us so much that he holds us in existence from moment to moment! If he stopped thinking of us even for an instant we would vanish into nothingness! Do you understand what I am saying?"

As before, a hand went up. A man of about forty spoke. "I sure do!" he said, as he unbuttoned his shirt.

Opening the shirt enough to bare his skin a little, he continued in a loud voice, "You see these two marks here on my chest? That's where I was shot!" Then, pointing with his finger,

he continued. "Two .38 slugs caught me—one right here! And
the other right there! They both came out behind my shoulder!
That was eight years ago. And here I am, still walking around!
So when you say that God holds me in existence, I know for
sure that what you're saying is a fact!"

Truly, this man ministered to me by jolting me into
awareness that God is present to us on endless levels of understanding. His understanding of God as Sustainer had come
through the school of very hard knocks, whereas mine had
come by way of intellectual musings. Of the two viewpoints,
his might well have been the more transcendent.

The Prophet

People referred to him as "the Prophet." On a certain memorable night six of us, including the Prophet, met in the
chapel. As the readings and comments proceeded, it became
evident to all that the man was at least mildly demented. He
interrupted me and began to talk on and on. Holding his finger up in the manner of a sage teaching with great intensity,
he commented on the words of scripture. His thoughts became increasingly abstract and convoluted.

At the conclusion of one of the readings, he said: "When
reading that passage, you got to bear in mind, keep before
you, and retain in your memory that the writer of that passage was holding on to what of necessity he must grasp. He
himself was engaged in making society even more society. He
was situated where ideas enter a new realm, where they come
together, intermingle, and go apart. He was trying to reach us
by way of words, speaking to us as words in the cycles of life
become life!"

Some of the men started growing restless on hearing him
speak this way. Thus, my task quickly changed to that of
treating the man with dignity while at the same time terminat-
ing his run-on speech. Trying not to dismiss him as one whose

words were valueless, I worked in a comment about people honoring one another by being good listeners. Seemingly, the men understood what I meant and became more tolerant of the fellow.

The meeting ended on a positive note, with the men shaking hands and smiling. The Prophet stayed behind. Lingering awhile, he went on speaking to me until I finally told him I had to leave, for he was very long-winded. He left cheerfully, smiling and speaking disconnectedly in highly intellectual terms. I asked myself what the future might hold for him. Thankfully, places such as Ozanam Inn exist for good persons such as he.

Two weeks later he showed up again. As before, when he spoke he drifted from religion, to politics, to sports, to definitions of adultery, all in two minutes' time. Knowing better what to expect this time, I allowed him to go on until I caught a single statement of his with which I could agree. Interrupting him, I repeated that statement of his emphatically and with acclaim, then quickly gave others a chance to speak. The tactic worked well. In effect, what he had done was to teach me a new technique.

Listening to the Voice

Gathered together one night, eight of us began to philosophize a little about religion. One of the street men initiated the discussion.

"How do I know when God is speaking to me?" he asked. "I don't hear any voices talking to me."

"Well, let's think of it like this," I said. "I ask myself, why did I come here tonight? One thing you can be certain of is that I myself did not feel like coming here tonight! But I came anyway. And I doubt if any of you men felt like coming here to this session. Yet you are here."

Several nodded in agreement.

"That's true." one man said. "I felt like watching TV upstairs, but when you announced a Bible-sharing meeting, I changed my mind and walked into this chapel instead."

"Yeah!" another man agreed. "I was thinking of playing a game of checkers, but I also decided I ought to come here instead."

"That's it!" I exclaimed. "The word is 'ought'! I came here tonight because I understood I ought to come. And you, too—you showed up at this meeting because you understood you ought to come. Whenever we listen to what it is we ought to do, we're listening to the voice of God. Whenever we listen to what we feel like doing, we're listening to our own voice. God speaks to us through our understandings of 'ought'!"

I went on to tell them that I believed that this is what Jesus of Nazareth had habitually done. He kept asking himself what were the things that he ought to do and to say. He never stopped asking himself that question and so he was always listening to the "voice of his Father." We, too, must always do that if we are to know ourselves at our best. Several men nodded in agreement.

Bizarre Questions

Occasionally, a man of limited education ventures to ask a strange question or two during the Bible-sharing sessions.

"Now tell me," one man insisted. "What would you do if God came knocking at your door one day. What would you do if you opened your door and found him standing there and he told you to follow the devil? Would you obey him?"

"Sir, you're making an impossible assumption!" I responded. "God, who is all-good, all-loving, and all-truthful has already told us that we are not to follow the path of evil. You're assuming that God might contradict God when you speak that way. Your question implies that God is not reliable and, therefore, is less than God. Do you see what I mean?"

"Yeah, I guess you're right." he conceded. "But I thought I would ask anyway."

"It's okay that you asked," I said. "Your question gives us the chance to focus our attention on things of the spirit."

Reflecting afterwards on his strange question, and trying to listen with my so-called "third ear," I asked myself what he could possibly have been attempting to do when he spoke as he did in the presence of ten or so others. On thinking it over I concluded that he, perhaps like me sometimes, wanted to be in the limelight for a moment and gain some degree of recognition by posing a philosophical question. I saw then that his question was basically a plea for attention. It was as if he were saying, "Please recognize the truth that there is more to me than what meets the eye." Seen from this perspective, his question might actually have made sense.

A Truly Happy Person

One does, indeed, find poor attitudes and occasional ingratitude among street people. Psychologically, much of it seems to originate as a defense against total collapse from within. In contrast, however, one also discovers wonderful ladies and gentlemen among street people, and some with a deep spiritual sense.

A man about forty was present at my group meeting one evening. He sat in silence for a time, not as one having nothing to say but, rather, as a disciplined man who had much to say while awaiting his turn to speak. And, when his turn came, his words of wisdom made it a delight to listen to him. He spoke of something boundless and ethereal, yet definite and loving that he experienced within himself wherever he went. He described himself as a truly happy person.

"The presence of the Lord is an ongoing personal experience for me," he said. "Over and over, wherever I go, my awareness of God keeps me going!"

Several other street people agreed that they, too, had had the same experience.

This man's presence at the Inn that memorable night gave a touch of elegance and grace to our meeting.

The Man Who Had Been "Enslaved"

Street people often speak of Satan and the end of the world, and possibly with good reason. Many are survivors of terrible personal experiences.

Phil, a man about twenty-seven, had long dark hair, a fluffy beard, a puffy face, and a mild disposition. One day he entered the chapel where I happened to be meeting with five or six men for Bible sharing. Without uttering a word he eased himself into an empty chair, focused his eyes on the floor, sat with downcast eyes, and remained silent in spite of my greetings.

Then, after we had finished reading the Bible parable about the rich man and Lazarus, the members of the group began to share their thoughts. When it was Phil's turn to speak, he started talking about harboring traumatic memories from his recent past. He said he had been "enslaved" by members of a commune to which he had belonged far away out West.

"They operated a business that took in $30,000 a month," he explained. "Yet I barely got enough money to buy my clothes and repair my shoes. I smoked marijuana in order to overcome depression. Those people 'loved me to death' while putting me to work for fourteen hours a day as my so-called therapy."

We later came to understand that Phil was identifying himself with the biblical character, Lazarus, and identifying the leaders of the commune with the rich man in the scriptural passage about Lazarus. Several men in the chapel spoke out on Phil's behalf, encouraging him and asserting their belief that he had been dealt a harsh injustice.

At the end of the session Phil stayed on to talk with me for almost an hour. He seemed rather nervous, so we stood, we sat, and we walked while talking about what in life is good and true. We spoke about listening to the Spirit, and he wanted to know what he should do at those times when Satan spoke to him as, he insisted, Satan often did. I suggested that he focus exclusively on the Lord, explaining that as long as he kept his focus on the Lord, Satan would have no power over him. Then I proceeded to talk to him about how important it is to pray on an ongoing basis.

"Give the Lord thanks for everything good in your life," I said. "Thank him for your life, for your food, for your health, for your eyesight, for your mind, for the air that you breathe, for the bed in which you are resting, for the chair in which you are sitting, for the buttons on your shirt, for the telephone, for the water that you drink. Thank him for the blue of the sky, for the trees, the birds, the flowers, the door knobs, the shoe laces and the pencils that you use. Thank him for everything you see and touch and hear, and continue doing that all day long! Ask him to forgive those who gave you a raw deal, and to find a way of bringing them around to his kingdom!"

He responded in a positive way by shaking his head affirmatively in silence. Slowly he walked out of the chapel, entered the recreation room, glanced at the TV set, turned around as if dissatisfied with the featured program, ambled into the dorm, and fell into his bed for the night.

Personal Gifts

One evening, I led the discussions into passages from the letter of Paul to the Romans. Keeping in mind that people do best in what they love most to do, I tried to focus attention on people's natural abilities.

"When we do the things we love to do, we generally feel closer to God," I said. I then quoted words from Paul's letter to the Romans (12:6): "So we are to use our different gifts in accordance with the grace that God has given us. If our gift is to speak God's message, we should do it according to the faith that we have. If it is to serve, we should serve. If it is to teach, we should teach. If it is to encourage others, we should do so."

Then I invited them to mention their own personal gifts, stating the kind of work or hobby activities that draw them closer to the Lord.

"I do a good job in the yard," said a young man. "I like cutting grass, pulling up weeds, planting flowers, and training vines. I like working with green things, and I enjoy smelling them while I work."

"I'm a freight mover," said a small man who looked about fifty years old. "I move boxes around in a warehouse using a hand truck. I'm good at it. I really know what I'm doing, and I feel good about myself when I do it!

"I am a carpenter," said a thin man with a small mustache. "I like nailing things together."

"I bet you consider the grain in the wood and know how to nail boards without splitting them." I responded.

"Yes, indeed," he replied. "And it feels good just to stand back and look at what I've constructed after my work is done."

"I'm glad you mentioned that," I said. "It reminds us of something in the book of Genesis where it says that God 'looked' at what he created and saw that it was good."

Once I received a somewhat unusual response when asking those in the group to cite their talents. A Mexican—young, good-looking, and apparently quite strong—told us of his special gift.

"I'm a boule rider!" he said.

"A what?" somebody asked.

"A boule rider," he repeated. "I like to ride the boules!"

"You mean the bulls? You ride those wild bucking bulls we see at rodeos?"

"*Sí!*" he responded. His faced beamed. "People liked to watch me do that. They cheered and clapped, and that made me feel good. But I broke my hip and my leg, and the doctor told me never to ride another boule. Never!"

"I think you ought to listen to the doctor," an elderly man commented. "He's trying to tell you that you had better stop, or you'll really mess yourself up for life. If you like being around bulls, maybe you can find a job teaching others how to ride them. Maybe the broken bones you suffered will help you to be a good teacher."

"Maybe," he responded, nodding and smiling. "I must think about that. My head has not been right just lately. I need some time to get my life together once more."

His concluding statement was one I've often heard from street people. Truly, they are aware of their problems and abnormalities and look with hope toward circumventing them. How very difficult it must be for dreams such as theirs to one day come true.

The Occult

Occasionally I meet people—most of whom are young—who seem to have been involved in satanic cults. They quickly jolt me into realizing my limitations as a listener. They sometimes refer to specific evil spirits by strange names as if showing familiarity with them, even smiling at times when uttering those horrible, foolish syllables. As quickly as possible I try to change the subject, for I have little desire to entangle myself with talk about devils. Occasionally, too, an alcoholic speaks of overindulgence in terms of demons coming out of bottles.

"Those liquor bottles are full of demons!" one young man exclaimed. "As soon as you unscrew that cap on the bottle, those damn demons come out and swarm all over you. There's no way in this world you can stop drinking, because they take you over and make you want to keep on drinking!"

The tendency to blame evil spirits for one's misconduct is, I suppose, as old as the human race itself. I insist that people are weak, and that we need God's help to rise above our weaknesses. We rise above our weaknesses to the extent that we lose ourselves in God.

"Pray always!" I say. "Talk to God constantly in your heart. To the extent that we do this, there's no room for evil to become rooted in us, no place for it to take hold. Try to see God's presence everywhere—in every situation, in every person, in every thing, in every moment! Talk to God all day long!"

One day a man of about twenty-three began to relate a story about a satanic group sacrificing a human child. I told him I did not want to hear about it, as I found the idea itself sickening. And so he said nothing more.

Afterwards I had second thoughts about my response. Perhaps he needed to unload his burden by talking about it. Should I not have been open-minded enough to put my personal feelings on hold for the moment so as to address the needs of that man? Having brought four beautiful children into this world, however, I found it difficult to listen to him without relating his descriptions in some way to my own children.

I continued to reflect on this matter, and I eventually concluded that I had, perhaps, done the correct thing that night. For, by refusing to listen to stories of the occult, I had ministered to my own spiritual needs. If I am to effectively minister to people in need, I must acknowledge my own limitations and be humble enough to not take on what is beyond my power to handle.

A Near-Death Experience

There is no end of stories in the world of the homeless, some of the tales being strange and most unusual. While completing my Bible-sharing session in a six-man group one night, I asked if anyone had any final words to say before we ended. A hand went up.

"Yes, I want to say something," a thin, rather handsome man of about thirty-five exclaimed.

"You mentioned something about Jesus assuring his followers that their spirit would transcend death when their body dies. And you said how you imagine us saying to ourselves when meeting God face to face: 'This is what I have always wanted! This is what I have been searching for in everything I have ever done!'"

"Yes, I did indeed say that. I said it because I don't see how it could be otherwise."

"Well, I have something to say that is going to sound very strange to all of you who are here tonight. It's something that happened to me a few years ago. And it won't surprise me if you do not believe what I have to say. The strange fact is that I have already experienced death!"

"You WHAT?" someone asked.

"I said that I experienced death," he repeated, with a quiet smile.

"Explain what you mean," someone said.

"I was in a really bad car accident when I was twenty. I was almost decapitated. They took me to the hospital and the doctors worked on me and finally decided to give up because I had no pulse at all for a time. They put a sheet over my body and wheeled it off to their storage room. A little later one of the orderlies passed by and noticed some fresh-looking blood on the sheet and called the doctor. So they wheeled my body back into the operating room where a doc-

tor worked on me. He and a friend of his stayed with me for
seventy-two hours. Finally, my life signs seemed stable. But I
remained in a coma for three months. And then, at last, I re-
gained consciousness."

"Wow! What an experience!" someone muttered.

"Well, the strange thing about it was that it seemed like
my soul had left my body—but not completely. Somehow, I
could actually see those doctors working on my body, then finally giving up. I could see my family coming into that room
and being very upset over everything that was happening.
Even though I didn't have the use of my bodily eyes, I could
'see' everything that was going on. It was as if I saw it all in
a dream that was very, very real. I saw the whole works as if
I was apart from my body and looking back at it. The really
odd thing about it was that I felt that I could hold onto this
world if I wanted to. Or I could let go of this world. It was as
if the choice was mine and I just couldn't make up my mind.
My mother had died some years before, and it was as if she
was telling me not to let go just yet, because the family still
needed me."

"That's a very strange story," I commented. "And I have
heard of things like it before. Years ago I read a book entitled
Life after Life, which was written by a medical doctor who
went around collecting stories similar to yours, stories in
which patients who had been given up for dead afterwards
'came back' to life. He interviewed several of them to find out
whether there were experiences that they all had in common.
Have you ever read that book?" I asked.

"No, I haven't," he immediately responded, "but I have
heard of it. A friend told me about it."

"Well, I suggest you read it. I think you will discover
many things in that book that are very much like what we've
heard you saying tonight. Some of the people spoke of sens-
ing that they were in the presence of a kind of 'loving light'
and several of them associated that light with Jesus Christ.
Was your experience like theirs?"

"Well, yes and no," he said. "I don't recall seeing a light as such, but I was totally aware of the full presence of Jesus. It was as if I could see all of life, and the reason why I could do that was because of him."

"How did you feel about 'coming back' to this life?" I asked.

"Well, I wasn't too happy about it. I felt very strongly that I wanted to go the other way, but I was compelled to stay here because I was needed by others. I am thinking especially about my brother. He was a policeman. He was really broken up about my death. Months later I told him all about what I had seen, including having seen him crying over my body in the hospital. I told him exactly where he sat, what direction he had faced, and how he suddenly had walked out of that room. He couldn't believe it. Then he died a year later. So I feel that I helped get an important message to him before he died."

"You mean you believe that Jesus might have been trying to save your brother by way of what was happening to you?" I asked.

"Very definitely! You know, that fellow Jesus is really very slick!" he said. "He's so slick that he could charm the skin off a snake! And when it comes to saving people, it's unbelievable the extent to which he will go! He wasn't kidding when he spoke about leaving the flock to seek out the lost sheep."

"I'm not afraid to die anymore," he concluded. "I would just as soon die as live. I want to live now, not because I'm afraid of death, but because I want to help other people to see what I saw. I really feel today the way that Jesus the Lord felt, that I have been sent, and that I have a mission!"

Primitive Imageries

I have observed how certain people never seem to move beyond their childhood imageries. This became apparent one night as I spoke with a group of eleven men. Midway through the discussion one of them exclaimed: "I was taught as a child that everyone goes to hell."

I asked him to explain.

"Well, my mother told me that everyone is going to die. And when they die they are buried in the ground. And under the ground is where the devil lives."

As he spoke, it became apparent that he was utilizing the word "hell" in place of the word "grave." I think what he meant to say was that everybody will go to the grave someday.

"Do you really believe that devils live under the ground?" I asked.

"Well, I don't know. But that's what they told me when I was small."

His was the case of a fifty-year-old thinking as a ten-year-old would think, never venturing to obtain answers for himself. He seemed a good man, but so primitive were his imageries that I hardly knew what to say. Speaking up loudly, another man insisted that the world is evil.

"Look here!" he began. "We got the things of God, and we got the things of the world. Nobody can be a friend of God and a friend of the world at the same time!"

"Tell us more clearly what you mean," I said.

"If you want to be a friend of God, then you can't take part in politics, or television, or making money."

"Sir, I really don't agree with you," I replied. "I see many people on television talking about how good God is. And the Bible tells us that after creating the world God 'saw that it was good.' And as far as I am concerned, persons who love God are the very ones who ought to engage in worldly things so as to let the spirit of the Lord blossom out from every corner of creation."

"Yeah, and not all politicians are evil!" an African-American man added. "Look at Abraham Lincoln! He was an example of a politician who loved God and spoke with a fair amount of wisdom."

After this sharing session ended, a soft-spoken young man of about twenty remained in the chapel to speak privately with me.

"Deacon," he began, "I can't see why you let those men speak error in the chapel!"

"I do so because I think this is the best way I know for correcting error. Rather than suppressing the expression of error, I think we ought to allow that expression to come into the light and then replace the error with truth. Don't you agree?"

"Well, I don't know," he said with an air of doubt. He paused a second, then continued. "Deacon, things like what they were saying scare me. Can't you do something to make my heart feel better?"

"Well, thank you for telling me that," I said. "Now I know where you're coming from."

So I placed my hand on his head and prayed aloud for the Lord to console and reward him. The blessing I gave him seemed to move him deeply. As I ended my prayer, he stood up and hugged me tightly, saying that he loved me. Smiling brightly, he spoke of feeling safe and serene, at least for the night. I, too, was deeply moved and felt elated. At least for the night!

Signs from God

Many street persons believe rather strongly in direct signs from God. I was reminded of this when engaged in a conversation one night with a member of a fishing crew.

"You know," this man said, "I'm a deck hand on a shrimp boat. One thing I do not like is sitting around doing nothing while waiting for the fog to lift. We were marooned in the fog one day and I began praying for the fog to go away.

And, don't you know, within ten minutes a wind came up and blew the fog away!"

"That's wonderful that you would pray," I answered. "But I'm willing to bet that even if the fog hadn't lifted so quickly you would have been able to find some meaning in that, too. Maybe you would have seen the lingering fog as the Lord's way of asking more patience from you than you ordinarily show."

"Yeah, that's probably true," he said.

"So you see," I continued, "the wonderful thing about prayer is that it brings us to see ordinary situations in special ways. Sometimes it causes us to act like kids living in a wonderland. We see wonder in whatever is at hand. Do you understand what I mean?"

"Yeah! Yeah! Let me give you another example. I like to collect knick-knacks, like seashells, and rocks, and crucifixes. One day I needed money and decided to sell a big crucifix I had, but I wasn't sure I should do that because it was a thing of the Lord. Finally, I tucked it into my bag and took off on my motorcycle to sell it. Well, I got in a wreck on my way to the pawn shop. Don't you think that the Lord was preventing me from selling it?"

"Well, it sure looks like something prevented you from selling it. If your accident brought you to understand that the Lord was working on you, then I think that's great! Don't you think so?"

"Yeah! Yeah!" he said. "Yeah! That is great!"

The Man Who Visited Medjugorje

As mentioned earlier, I find it difficult to relate to self-righteous Bible-waving persons. But I also find it difficult to relate to the self-righteous of my own religion who attach themselves to personal cults of devotion and wish to impose their beliefs on others.

One man in particular comes to mind. When I arrived in the chapel that night to await the arrival of the others for my sharing session, I found this young man already there, praying the rosary while smiling peacefully. He was in his early twenties.

"Do you all say the rosary here?" he asked.

"As far as I know, it is done by some persons privately, but not done in groups," I answered.

"Well, it's crucial for it to be done, you know!"

Others were entering the chapel by then. Soon the scripture readings commenced, and I invited individuals to comment on the words just read. When his turn came to speak, the young man mentioned having visited Medjugorje, the Yugoslavian village where Mary, the mother of Jesus, was said to be appearing. Smiling, he spoke of his peaceful experiences there and about God wanting all persons to experience inner peace. It became apparent that he wanted to speak at length about Medjugorje, a topic that clearly had nothing to do with the scripture passages we were reflecting on that night.

Because of him, I had to strictly chair the session lest he divert attention from the biblical topics under consideration. I was quietly determined not to allow him to take over the meeting. An hour later I ended the session as usual with a prayer. As I spoke the closing words, the young man said in a loud voice:

"Let's all of us make the sign of the cross!"

Embarrassed somewhat, and realizing that most of the men there were not Catholics, I said, "Whoever wishes to make the sign of the cross may do so on his own."

After the others had left the chapel, the young man went into a tirade, criticizing me for not insisting that everyone make the sign of the cross. He grew rather sharp in his words.

"You know, Satan has a hold on you!" he said. "You chose not to lead the men in making the sign of the cross!"

"Aren't you judging me rather harshly?" I asked. "After all, I did lead the men in prayer, didn't I? I might not have done it your way, but I just finished encouraging the men to communicate with God all day long. And you're telling me that Satan has a hold on me because I did not insist that they, a mixed group of Christians, make the sign of the cross at your insistence?"

"You have a lot of hidden hatred in you," he replied, his smile momentarily vanishing.

"Maybe so. I guess we all do. Yet, I do love my religion, sir, which seems to be the same as yours. But I sure as heck am not going to try forcing it on others. Religious faith, if it is to be genuine, must come about as response to an invitation. I guess we disagree on that. But anyway, I wish you good luck wherever you go."

"Did you say 'luck'? 'Luck' is not the word!" he corrected me. "'Luck' is from Satan! 'Blessings' are from God!"

"I don't wholly agree with you," I responded. "Nothing in creation—not even luck—is separate from God who created all things. But, anyway, I wish you God's best, whatever that might mean to you and to me. Good-bye for now."

He showed up again a month later, at which time he was in a more tranquil mood. When his time came to speak, he mentioned that he had been hospitalized for mental illness but was now cured.

Voices of Angels

A fatigued-looking, sleepy-eyed man about thirty-five joined our sharing session one night. His tight-fitting faded green shirt featured but a single button holding it together across his hairy chest. He listened as we discussed the biblical readings and then at one point he stood up and addressed the group.

"I'm a man who lived in the 'fast lane' for almost ten years." he said. "I had plenty of money at first. I could buy just about anything I wanted."

He went on to speak of how much he had liked wearing gold jewelry, driving high-performance automobiles, dating amorous women, and dealing drugs.

"Then I got into using drugs myself," he continued. "I ended up needing money so bad that I had to sell what I owned. I lost everything and began stealing from my family. I took their VCR, their television, and their new microwave oven, which I sold for almost nothing to get me a fix. Then they threw me out of the house," he said.

"Me, too!" another man said. "I done the same!"

"And me too!" a third man chimed in.

"But then I went to my mother," the man explained. "I told her I had done wrong. I asked her to help me straighten out and she agreed to do it. Now I'm getting ready to return to my home, and I'm trying very hard to stay away from crack."

There was a moment of silence and then he added, "I wish that I had listened to my mother from the beginning. Now that I've come so far down the road I'm able to look back and see that her words—even her loud words—were like the voice of an angel trying to reach me!"

"In many situations," I reminded him, "the voices of our parents—especially our mothers—are like those of messengers from the Lord. Often we have only to listen to our parents in order to know what the Lord wants."

I said this, however, in a careful sort of way, mindful that it is not always true. For, sad to say, certain parents in today's society are themselves very afflicted.

The Man Who Wouldn't Hurt a Flea

A small bald-headed man of about sixty showed up on a spring evening, one of the six people at my Bible-sharing session. He was disfigured by a lengthy, unbandaged cut extending from the edge of his left eye all the way over his head to the back of his right ear. No one dared ask him about the hideous-looking cut that featured numerous stitches along its entire length. In spite of its grotesque appearance, he sat among us very much at ease, smiling and speaking mildly as if there were nothing at all unusual in his appearance. His overall demeanor seemed to indicate that a new chapter had begun in a life temporarily marred by a bad experience. I saw him the following week and noticed that the cut was well on its way to healing. Then, as before, he was smiling as he entered the dining hall for a sandwich.

A month later I got the news that he had been murdered. Somewhere in the boondocks far from the city his body had been found in an abandoned warehouse. Those who told me of this shook their heads in disbelief, emphatically stating that he was a man who wouldn't hurt a flea, asking themselves why anyone would ever want to kill someone like him.

Hanging On to the Vine

Many street persons navigate their world in desperation, placing their faith in God. "I tell you, Deacon, it's rough out there!" one of them said. "I feel as if the friendship of the Lord is the only thing I have left. It's like being in the woods and getting stuck in quicksand. Sometimes I feel like I'm sinking up to my ears. The Lord is like a vine that is dangling down from a tree limb, and I'm holding on tightly so as not to sink. If ever I let go of that vine, I'll have nothing whatever in this world to look forward to."

6

WANDERERS AND THE COMMUNITY

It is heartening that in recent times the news media are paying more attention to the homeless than in previous decades. In addition to television news stories on the homeless, one finds occasional newspaper articles addressing their plight.

On January 22, 1996, the New Orleans *Times-Picayune* ran a story entitled, "Florida Shelter Might Be an Inspiration." The article described an apparently successful Orlando, Florida, public shelter for the homeless that was said to have "nearly eliminated the problem of transients roaming the business district." In Orlando, where tourism is a prime industry, concern runs high over the negative effects of homeless persons in the streets. The shelter described in the article was built at a cost of $350,000 from Orlando's Downtown Development Board. Known as the Pavilion, the facility offers help and provides food, shelter, showers, bedding, counseling, medical assistance, and legal and employment aid. Since the shelter's opening, there have been far fewer transients showing up at tourist attractions.

In early 1997 the following article, authored by *Times-Picayune* staff writer James Gill, was printed in the New Orleans paper:

City Wrong on Charitable Act Case

It seems that the City of New Orleans was determined to make a complete ass of itself, with the media on hand to record the spectacle, when Julie Bourbon's case came up in Municipal Court Monday.

Bourbon, accused of performing charitable acts, had appeared for trial a few weeks ago, but prosecutors were granted a delay. It seemed odd that they were not prepared, for the facts were not in dispute.

Bourbon was caught red-handed distributing food to the vagrants of Lafayette Square in alleged violation of city ordinances. She has been doing so regularly for five years as a member of Loyola University's Community Action Program. What we have here is a career criminal.

Repeat offenders are a dime a dozen at Loyola where students tend to be familiar with the Bible and therefore have heads full of subversive ideas. Although Bourbon was the only one booked, a regular gang of students would descend on the square a couple of times a week armed with sandwiches, fruit, chips and soft drinks...

Finally, appearing in New Orleans's *Times-Picayune* on March 27, 1997, and written by staff writers Susan Finch and Coleman Warner, there was this article:

Twelve Million Sought to Shift Homeless Out of Quarter
Complex to Offer an Array of Services

Prompted partly by humanitarian concern, partly by a desire to get homeless people out of the city's key tourist and business centers, New Orleans is closing in on a plan to build a huge multiservice center for the homeless on a nine-acre complex a few blocks from the Superdome.

The complex, proposed for a site along Poydras Street near the Broad Street overpass, would provide food, sleeping space, medical care, a chapel and a small park...

So it was said when enthusiasm ran high. A director was appointed who would lead a campaign to collect $12 million to build and equip a compound for serving men, women, and children at the site. Was the plan ever put into action?

No. It became like a fruit that died on its vine. Then came Hurricane Katrina on August 29, 2005.

Aftermath of Katrina

Considered the greatest natural disaster ever to strike the United States, Hurricane Katrina approached with top winds of 165 mph that decreased somewhat before making landfall. The hurricane did not strike New Orleans directly, but grazed its eastern edge.

As it happened, the greatest damage to the city resulted not directly from the winds, but rather from the collapse of the floodwalls of certain canals used to collect waters from the city and pump them into nearby Lake Pontchartrain. Katrina's strong surge caused the backward flow of water from the lake into these canals, where substandard floodwalls broke. Water poured out from the canals, flooding over 75 percent of the city.

In November, 2008, Clarence Adams, Sr., assistant administrator of Ozanam recalled: "Immediately before the hurricane's arrival we closed the Inn at noon and our entire staff made their way to the Superdome. In and around this huge facility were gathered some 35,000 people—mostly poor African Americans who were stranded because buses and trains were not operating. Helicopters were arriving there with individuals who had been rescued from rooftops and tree limbs. It was a terrible place to be, as food was scarce, electricity was off, and there was little police protection. Mothers with small children were especially vulnerable."

It was fortunate that no flooding occurred at Ozanam Inn as the building was situated on ground rather close the Mississippi River. But for a time, lack of electricity, gas, drinking water, and other necessities made it impossible to operate normally. Almost every store was closed, and many weeks went by before workers began returning to the city. Without electricity, refrigeration was non-existent and, except for canned foodstuff and such, much of the food throughout the city became spoiled.

After Katrina a large number of homeless encamped in Duncan Plaza, their tents and bags situated within sight of the mayor's City Hall office. They refused to move unless suitable places were located for them. This tactic of theirs seemed to work, and slowly their numbers at that place decreased as various unused apartments were located for them by city officials.

The collapse of the public health system was a calamity of the first order. Many medical facilities were flooded out of operation, and New Orleans was left with one-half of its hospitals. Charity Hospital, the second largest public hospital in the nation, suffered extensive damage and, along with its network of community clinics, was put out of operation. To this day, more than three years later, the facility has remained closed. In all, four sizeable hospitals have not yet been able to reopen.

Many severely mentally ill citizens are returning to the city and the mental health crisis today is the most socially impacting byproduct of Hurricane Katrina. There has been an increase in suicides and post-tramatic stress disorder since Katrina along with a severe shortage of nurses and hospital beds. Calls for help for the mentally ill are now being handled by the New Orleans Police Department Crisis Unit.

In 2007, two years after Katrina, hundreds of homeless citizens were still encamped beneath the elevated Interstate 10 Highway passing through the downtown area. Many slept on the pavement there and sheltered themselves by living under improvised plastic covers or inside large cardboard boxes. They begged for money and visited soup kitchens and shelters where food was given out.

Ozanam was able to reopen within three months after the hurricane, and for some time it was the only adult shelter that was up and running in the city. "In the beginning we had to operate for a time with only half of our usual staff back at work," says Clarence Adams. "Operating our kitchen were three cooks in place of the previous six. And these were cooking for twice the number of pre-Katrina street persons. With overcrowded conditions within the Inn, many people were sleeping outside in the yard next to the building. In time, a slow but steady recovery took place and Ozanam Inn is presently back to near-normal operation. This means that approximately 600 meals are served each day and 96 men per night are now being accommodated—with 125 per night in freezing weather. Medical school students show up almost daily as they did before the hurricane to treat ailing clients, and a medical doctor named Ted Borgman volunteers to see our unfortunates during part of his Saturday off-duty days."

In the aftermath of Katrina rebuilding of the city has been slow and, of course, the poor and those on the fringes of society have suffered the most. There are signs of hope, though, such as a new service called "The Rebuild Center," where the homeless and the working poor have access to a range of services including showers, laundry, food, mail, and telephones, as well as legal and immigration services. The center opened on September 9, 2007, and, with its emphasis on support and dignity, it provides a safe and welcoming place for people looking to rebuild their lives.

"They Hit It Lucky"

The evening sun hung low in the sky as I came to Ozanam earlier than usual one day in order to linger outside with the street people before the doors opened. A motley group of men stood silently in front of the hospice. One of them approached me, looking quite upset.

"I saw something today that made my blood boil!" he said.

"What did you see?"

"An hour ago a bunch of us were standing here at the front door. A big tour bus pulled to a stop right there across the street. And—if you can believe this—a bunch of people in that air-conditioned bus aimed their cameras at us. They were smiling among themselves and pointing at us. It was as if they were at the zoo, taking pictures of animals. I felt like slitting the tires of that bus and making them all walk home!

"Those well-dressed bastards!" he continued. "They hit it lucky in life. They take their nice vacations. Then they come here and park and stare at us and act as if they're better than us because they have jobs and saved their money. I wanted to kick them all in their butts!"

I found it difficult to adequately answer him because I, myself, had at one time harbored a disdain for people such as he. I made no mention of this to him, yet in my heart I knew I was not really so far removed from those he criticized with such severity—and with such good reason.

Those Who Take Advantage

Almost unbelievably, there are persons who unfairly take advantage of street people. In addition to distilling firms that sometimes manufacture low-quality cheap liquor that makes people sick, there are those who prey on street people for the little money they sometimes have. Those who take advantage like this include some owners of small hotels and employment agencies.

One night, my co-worker Don told me about an experience he had had. On arriving at the Inn one evening, he was introduced to an elderly married couple, seventy-five or so years old, who were asking for assistance in finding an inexpensive room where they could spend the night together. Having been in the streets for several months, they had not once slept together in privacy during all of that time. They sought a place where, as they said, they could "really hug each other" for a change.

Hoping to open for them new possibilities where dead-ends had previously existed, Don phoned a small hotel listed with the Inn. The owner promised that they could sleep together that night. On hearing the news, the faces of the man and woman lit up and their eyes twinkled. Encumbered with suitcase and knapsack, they shuffled off toward the promised lodgings at the hotel several blocks away.

In a follow-up move, Don visited the hotel the next day. A middle-aged man who seemed highly pleased with himself received him coolly but nevertheless agreed to show him where the elderly couple had slept. He was ushered into a very large room. Spread out on the floor were several double-size mattresses.

"You mean to say that this is where they slept?" Don asked.

"Yeah. They had the chance they asked for, to sleep together. They slept right there on that double mattress," the man said.

"But they had no privacy!" Don said. "And—"

"Look, man," the owner interrupted, "I'm not in the business of guaranteeing privacy! I guarantee a place to sleep, not privacy!"

Deeply disappointed, Don left. In telling me the story, he said, "The instant I saw the place I sensed a calamity of a sort. Several poorly dressed, unhealthy-looking men were plodding along at work in his yard and around his hotel. It's true that I do not know what kind of an understanding he had with them, but it seemed to me that the hotel owner might have been pushing them for all he could get out of them. Henry, you would have to meet the fellow to know what I mean. He seemed to operate three-fourths of the way up the hyena scale! He reminded me of the type of person that Thomas Merton referred to when he wrote: 'Blinded by his own self-ishness, he cannot even see that he is blinded.'"

Don's story reminded me of another one I had heard earlier from a street man. "There's a man in Oil Town who milks unemployed people like me and takes them for all they've got," he had said. "He operates an employment agency and owns a motel and a restaurant next door."

"How does he operate?" I asked.

"Well, let's say you drive up to his place and ask him to find you employment on the oil rigs. He promises to get you a job within a few days and puts you up at his motel for a price. It turns out to be a long wait, but he keeps you hopeful that a job will come 'just any day now.' It becomes like gambling. You take a chance and stay there waiting, and finally you run out of money."

"What then?"

"Then he decides to allow you to stay longer provided you mortgage your automobile to him. You decide to take the risk. Two weeks later you lose your car! He's a relative of the sheriff, so the sheriff comes and seizes your car."

"This is beginning to really smell!"

"But wait! There's more! In his generosity he decides to allow you to stay several more nights on condition that you agree to pay him what you owe when your job comes through. And the job finally does come through. Hooray! You're happy over it, but you're also up to your ears in debt with him. While smiling, he insists that you sign over to him a certain amount of your future paychecks (and that amount includes interest) before he tells you the name of the offshore drilling company that's willing to hire you. He also insists that you sign a paper appointing him as your ongoing, active employment agent (at a very high fee), the man who keeps his eyes open in search of even better jobs than the one he just found for you."

"Oh, God! What a way to be crucified!"

"So, when you get paid, your check (according to the agreement you signed when you were down and out) goes to him before it goes to you. And he milks it for over two-thirds of what you've earned! You get to figuring it out and discover that he will be doing this to you for another eight months before you can get your head above water! Before you can own a car again! So it'll take you eight months just to get back to where you were when you first met him!"

I was appalled by this story, and I decided to inform Louisiana's attorney general of it in person, giving as many specifics as I could. Whether or not anything was ever done about it, I shall probably never know.

Trouble from Neighbors

A mood of intrigue pervaded Ozanam Inn when I arrived one evening.

"Have you heard?" a crewman asked.

"Heard what?"

"About the police! They're closing in on us!"

"You've got to be kidding!"

Little by little I learned the nature of the problem.

Neighboring businessmen were upset, and possibly with good reason. Several people were insisting that Ozanam Inn move its operations to some place other that its Camp Street location, only eight blocks from Canal Street, the wide avenue running through the prime business section of New Orleans. Ozanam was in a second- or third-class business area. However, massive new office buildings were then under construction along the wide avenue known as Poydras Street, only four blocks away. It seemed clear that future business expansion was destined to flow in the direction of Ozanam.

As it happened, men, women, and children came to Ozanam and stood in line for meals in mid-afternoon. A neighboring businessman became concerned over this line, which sometimes extended along the sidewalk in front of his place. He insisted that prospective customers of his were intimidated by the street people standing in line. Specifically, customers were afraid to cut across the line and enter his door. He also accused the street people of using foul language and urinating on his property. I asked Steven, Ozanam's director, about their concern, and this is what he told me:

"In response to a complaint once, the police closed in shortly before meal time and rounded up 108 street persons! They frisked them and took them away in paddy wagons.

"The following morning an assistant to the mayor phoned me about the incident. One of those street persons, a black man who was blind, had filed a complaint that the police had violated his civil rights. We were furious about it because, basically speaking, most of those people had done nothing other than stand in line while awaiting a mid-afternoon meal. I argued that the businessmen, on finding that they could not legally bring the Inn to close its doors, were trying to harass the street people away from its doors and put Ozanam out of business.

"The outcome of the phone conversation was that a meeting took place. It was attended by the presidents of the Ozanam Inn board and the St. Vincent de Paul organization, the director of Ozanam, the assistant police precinct commander, and the mayor. The meeting was amicable. The mayor fully acknowledged the long-time charitable works of the St. Vincent de Paul Society and the Ozanam staff. He mentioned that in his opinion the police raid should not have taken place. He insisted, however, that the police nevertheless had to respond to legitimate complaints of the community.

"The Ozanam Inn group agreed with much of what he said. The outcome of the meeting was that we arranged to station one of our staff members on the sidewalk in front of Ozanam in order to maintain order prior to meal time and bed time. The staff member would make sure that those waiting would line up in single file and against the fence, giving plenty of room to passersby on the sidewalk. He would especially insist that no derogatory or sexually debasing remarks be uttered by the street people, particularly when women were passing by."

"Protection Services"

The assigning of a religious brother on the sidewalk outside Ozanam Inn greatly defused a problem of community complaints. Nevertheless, a few more incidents did occur. Steven described one such incident, this one involving the police. Steven said he felt that the problem in this and certain other cases had more to do with individual police officers rather than with their commanders.

A month or two after the meeting with the mayor, Steven was told that a police car had pulled up in front of the Inn and its officers had ordered the street people there to place their hands against the wall. The officers then proceeded to frisk and search the people. The intent appeared to be to frighten them away. This had happened for several nights before Steven became aware of it. So on hearing about it, he began watching for it. Sure enough! One night he saw a police cruiser pull up in front of the Inn. Two officers got out and made the four or five street persons present lean against the wall.

Dressed in his white religious habit, Steven walked out of the Inn and stood there watching the officers, whose backs were toward him. One of the officers then turned around and caught sight of him.

"Oh, Brother, how are you doing tonight?"

"I'm doing all right!" Steven replied. "But what is this procedure of yours that you go through every night with these men?"

The younger officer seemed a little embarrassed. He stuttered and stammered a little. But the elder officer replied, "We're doing this for your protection, Brother!"

"You're doing what for my protection?" Steven asked.

"We check them out for weapons," the officer replied. "We don't want to see you brothers get hurt!"

"Well, that's awfully decent of you, Officer," Steven replied, "but if they have anything resembling a weapon, we ourselves make them check it in with us before going upstairs for the night. And, by the way, Officer, how many weapons have you found on them while searching them?"

"Well, we really haven't found any weapons on them," he replied.

"And may I ask you another question? This seems to have been going on now for about a week in front of Ozanam Inn, and it intimidates the street people. Tell me, do you also perform this service at night time for the other refuges—the Salvation Army and the Baptist missions, for example? Or is it only here on Camp Street? Do you provide this service exclusively for us?"

The elder officer became indignant.

"Well, we've never been asked to do this at the Baptist mission," he said.

"And who, may I ask, requested that you do this over here at this Catholic mission?" Steve inquired.

"Well, nobody really asked us," he said.

"Then why are you doing it here and not there?" Steve asked. "Something sounds strange about this. I know that the Camp Street businessmen have been pressuring us to keep these people away. Would that have anything to do with your showing up here? I want to get to the bottom of this. May I have your names?"

When neither officer would give me his name, Steven told them he had noted the number of their car. Filled with indignation and muttering to each other, they got into their cruiser, slammed the doors, and drove away. And, lo, that marked the end of their "protection services." Steven felt reasonably certain that they had done this on their own without having been ordered to do so from above.

In time, the problem of street people loitering in front of the Inn was eased when the St. Vincent de Paul Society purchased (at a very high cost) an empty lot adjacent to the Inn. The added land enabled Ozanam to absorb the people off the street and sidewalk. It allowed the homeless, while waiting for meals, to congregate behind a tall brick fence in an area within which were portable toilet facilities.

From a Practical Point of View

Having related these incidents, Steven then made it clear that the Inn also had friendly encounters with the police. He went on to give me an example.

One morning a knifing occurred a block or two away on Magazine Street. Covered with blood from head to toe, the victim staggered past several business places and barely made it to Ozanam, the only nearby place he felt would help him. The staff there, of course, immediately called for police and ambulance.

An old-timer, a lieutenant, showed up along with the ambulance. On arriving, the medics went to work on the victim right away. They found five deep stab wounds in him, from groin to neck. On turning him over, they discovered that the knife itself was buried up to its handle in his back. The man's pulse was zero. With a single sweep of her shears, a woman medic cut off his pants. They quickly replaced his pants with special rubberized trousers of a sort. On being inflated with air, the trousers helped restore some degree of blood pressure to the man's body.

It happened that one of the Ozanam crewmen, who had been a medic and an acquaintance of the ambulance team before he had taken to the streets, joined in to help. Working smoothly as a trained team, they administered IVs to the victim. The Ozanam crewman knew exactly what to do, and we were proud of him!

The police radioed news of the situation to other cruisers. Near Poydras Street and all along the route to the hospital, traffic was halted. They made it to Charity Hospital in record time. The man was rushed into the emergency room and, after receiving medical treatment at the hospital, he recovered. Amazingly, we spotted him standing in our food line only two weeks later! We learned that he had been stabbed by a drunken "friend." The violence stemmed from an earlier contest of some sort between the two in which the friend had been made to feel that he was someone of lesser importance. On later becoming drunk, the friend recalled his resentments and turned into a savage killer. To our knowledge, he was never prosecuted. The victim probably forgave him and just kept going. It would not be surprising to see them peacefully walking together again. Such are some of the street people.

While all that excitement was going on in front of the Inn, Steven remarked to the lieutenant, "I suppose incidents like this must be 'pains in the butts' for you fellows!"

"Not really." he said. "Let me ask you, how many street men sleep here at night?"

"About eighty or so." Steven answered. "More in the winter when it happens to be exceptionally cold outside."

"Well, think of it this way," the officer said. "Speaking not as a Christian from the point of view of compassion but, rather, from the strictly practical point of view of a police officer, that's eighty or so men you have taken off the streets. That's eighty or so fewer men whom we as police officers will have to worry about tonight. I really think you're doing the city a very great service!"

Problems of Homeless Women

I asked one of the Ozanam Inn administrators, Joseph, about street women—how did they fare?

"Not very well," he responded, and went on to tell me about several cases.

"Susan was an educated woman from Kentucky. After breaking up with her husband, she came to New Orleans, hoping that one of her children here would help her. She was not an alcoholic, and she hoped to find a job. But before she could land a job, her funds ran out, and she began coming to Ozanam for meals. This led to her being spotted by a man who afterwards raped her. Emotionally broken, Susan discontinued her efforts at finding a job. She no longer trusted anyone. The last time I saw her was some eight months ago, and at that point she was sleeping in doorways and hoping for the best.

"Concern over being raped, of course, is very high among women who are living on the streets. A lovely young woman named Linda comes to mind. Linda (who happened to be slightly crippled) had been raped several times, and we don't know what can be done about it. Now she is afraid of everyone. We recently gave her a blanket but she told us that she is afraid to come to the Inn, even to stand in line for a meal. She feels that it is too easy for street men to spot her and afterwards follow her. We haven't seen her in weeks. But we heard that she has been in touch with a couple of friends who are helping to look after her.

"And I remember Jessica, an attractive middle-aged woman. In my opinion she was schizophrenic—nice one day, horrible the next, and a perpetual chain smoker. We tried contacting her family about her, and her mother spoke with her on the phone. Still, Jessica wanted no close relationship with her family. One man after another picked her up, and she was eventually sent to jail. There, too, she was violent and abusive, so her family had her committed to a mental institution where she apparently received proper treatment and medication. A year later she phoned me. Sounding like a different person, she expressed profound gratitude for the move that took her to a hospital where she was treated and afterwards placed in a half-way house.

"And then there was a woman named Connie. She had been coming to Ozanam to eat, but she and her boyfriend were on drugs. They devised a system for robbing people. I actually saw it happen once. He would grab the victims from behind while she quickly frisked them for their money. Connie and her boyfriend were caught and jailed. After leaving jail they did it again and were imprisoned once more. Finally they were released, but with a solemn warning that should another robbery take place, they would be imprisoned for years. The threat seems to have sobered them, as they are both off drugs at present and both have full-time jobs."

Street women with small children pose special problems. Such was the case with Evelyn, a woman in her thirties who stopped at the Inn asking for shelter.

"We're sorry, but we're not allowed to take in women at Ozanam. It's strictly for men," she was told.

On being asked about local relatives, she mentioned that she had a brother and two sisters-in-law living in town.

"How about phoning them and asking them to take you and the children in for the night?" Joseph asked. "Tell them we'll drive you out to their place."

She adamantly refused, giving us the impression that she was on very poor terms with her relatives. Joseph then phoned more than twenty places—hospices, shelters, inexpensive motels. All said they were filled.

"We can't simply put them out on the street in this rain and chilly darkness, Joseph!" I exclaimed.

So I called home. My wife recommended one last refuge which, as it turned out, consented to taking Evelyn and the children in for one night. Immediately, I drove them the ten miles to that place where, as it happened, a Christmas party for children was going on. Someone stepped into the hall and invited the woman's children to the party. Their faces lit up and it was evident that they were in good hands, at least for that night.

One night at a time! What a way to live!

Loyola Shelters the Homeless

On a memorable occasion before the year was two weeks old, an intense cold front moved into New Orleans. Crowds of people arrived at Ozanam Inn looking for shelter, but the numbers were more than double what the facility could handle. Someone from the Inn phoned my university, asking if we might be able and willing to absorb the overflow. Several minutes later an answer arrived. Indeed, the university was willing to help.

Campus security officers supervised arrangements on the first floor of the Monroe Science Complex building, where for two consecutive nights thirty or more homeless persons slept on the carpeted floor and utilized the very clean rest rooms. Coffee and doughnuts were served in the mornings, after which the street people would leave for the day. Their presence on campus during those nights interfered in no way with school activities, especially since the students were at the time away from school on academic mid-year vacation.

Parish Outreach

Hilton, my former mentor in clinical pastoral training, eventually became the pastor of my parish. Having worked in prison ministry in the past, he understood unfortunates and encouraged me to continue working with the homeless. The plight of the poor seemed to haunt him, and he wanted our parish to help them, even if only on a limited basis. He asked me to reorganize the parish St. Vincent de Paul group, to expand its membership and increase the parishioners' awareness of the poor. Under the energetic leadership of their president, a very dedicated woman, the group opened up new dimensions of ministry.

Members began to receive street people at the front door of the parish center, providing them with food, bus tokens, and supermarket coupons. This was unprecedented—nothing like it had ever happened before in our parish. However, problems soon developed.

Word gets around fast among the homeless. It did not take long for the needy, including drifters, to come our way even from far-flung corners of the city. The coupons, which were redeemable at local supermarkets, were in great demand —actually in greater demand than the food we gave out.

Most of the needy were appreciative of what we did for them. However, certain cantankerous individuals were ever-demanding of more than their share. A typical comment would be: "Well, I've donated to the church all my life. Why can't they donate to me now that I need money?"

The fact that a certain poorly dressed man was seen driving up in a Cadillac before taking his place in line for food coupons bothered the pastoral staff. One day a man who had stopped by for food ran his automobile into a nearby culvert. The car remained there for two weeks, its rear end tilted skyward. Although complaints were not received, the pastoral staff began to sense that, realistically speaking, some of our callers were of such character that they might one day molest a student at our nearby elementary school, or possibly harm a parent.

Fearing that the situation might be getting of hand, the St. Vincent group chose to alter their policy. They eliminated the food coupons after having learned that some people might be selling them and then using the money to buy liquor. The new plan called for donating small packages of food and toilet articles at the front door. Mothers with young children were especially favored. After the plan was revised, the numbers of street persons coming to the center fell dramatically. Having discovered their limitations, the St. Vincent group nevertheless chose to keep the front doors open and did what they thought to be wise.

Shortly after discontinuing the food coupons, the St. Vincent group became directly involved at Ozanam Inn, but on a limited basis. Approximately four times a year they visited

Ozanam to prepare a Sunday meal for the street people. They purchased the food, cooked it, and served the people on the scene. Although the St. Vincent group's work was only one of the parish ministries, the parish as a whole appeared to profit from their efforts, and morale seemed to soar in proportion to their involvement with the poor.

Benefactors

Most of the street people who come to Ozanam are profoundly grateful for the services they receive there. Some ask about the organization and operation. I inform them of the St. Vincent de Paul Society, the persons who staff the Inn, and the numerous unseen benefactors, some of whom are quite wealthy. I point out that some affluent persons manage to remain relatively unspoiled. Such people think of themselves as stewards of the Lord who will one day render an account of their spending to their Master—and contributing to reducing the sufferings of the homeless represents an important part of that accounting.

Those who are unable to become personally involved at the hospices can, and indeed do, help with prayer and financial contributions. People who support the efforts of others to enhance the lot of the homeless deserve high praise.

Steven mentioned to me one evening that he always takes delight in showing benefactors how their money is being used. "I repeatedly tell them," he said, "'Without you, we're out of business! We might have a very fine building with shiny floors. But unless we have food for three hundred breakfasts and six hundred dinners each day; unless we have a room full of clothes and shoes to dress the men who are looking for jobs; unless money is coming in to pay the $2,000 monthly electric bill and the $1,500 monthly gas bill so that we can cook the food, heat the water for showers, and warm the place itself in the winter; unless we have these things—we're out of business! Very definitely, we are dependent on you!'"

7

BREAD ON THE WATERS

Someone once said: "Cast your bread upon the waters, and it will come back to you buttered." That is certainly what I have observed and personally experienced all through my years of working with street people. I have been deeply moved by the stories I have heard, the generosity and compassion I have witnessed, the tangible signs of God's mercy touching not only the lives of those I have met but also, through them, my own life.

A Lesson in Prayer

Many street persons pray quite actively. For them, friendship with God is often their sole remaining link with happiness. On entering the chapel one night I found a young man kneeling on the carpet immediately in front of the altar. Facing a large crucifix over the altar he was chanting aloud a series of prayerful invocations:

> *Bless the people who read your Bible, Father!*
> *Help me to find a job and go to work, Father!*
> *Take care of my father; take care of my mother, Father!*
> *Forgive me my sins; help me to pray, Father!*
> *Make me strong; make me faithful, Father!*

As he chanted, his voice dropped half an octave every time he uttered the word "Father."

He also prayed: *Send the people to hell who do not want to listen to you, Father!*

I made a mental note to speak to him about that final invocation, to suggest that he pray, *Find a way to convert those people who seem to be lost, Father!* However, the opportunity for me to do that did not arise until later, at which time it slipped my mind. My fault!

Then, taking a lesson from the young man, I said my own prayer:

Next time, help me remember, Father!

The Man Who Put Aside His Hatred

When I first met Frank, he was working as a crewman at Ozanam. I use his real name here because, shortly before his death, he gave me permission to do so when telling his story to others.

Frank, who was about sixty years old, was at that time working on electrical appliances and junction boxes throughout the three-story Inn. Blue-hued veins were prominent on the backs of his hands. His face was thin, and when looking him over I couldn't help thinking of World War II British Field Marshall Montgomery. Frank was well-spoken and obviously well read. In time the two of us grew to be friends. One August day he related his story to me while relaxing after supper.

"I grew up in New England," he began. "Shortly before World War II, I went north and joined the Canadian Army. I was a kid looking for adventure. Well, I certainly found my adventure! A year later, while still a teenager, I was on the beach at Dunkirk in France, with Nazi tanks advancing on my unit. That was in May 1940, and I'll never forget it!

"As the Nazis commenced their scouting operation, I was one of several men hidden in the forest near the beach who fired ground cannons at them. We did that in a planned rapid-fire sequence for the purpose of deceiving them into thinking that they were being fired at by hidden Allied tanks. In reality, the British had no tanks at all. But the trick seemed to work, at least in delaying the Germans from sending their tanks toward the beach.

"On the beach we were strafed by their Messerschmitt planes, which came in low and fast. I dug a foxhole beneath the wreck of an old truck. I jumped in and curled up to make myself as small as possible. The water in the hole was up to my neck, so I couldn't go any deeper. I have never been so scared in my life! Men were falling dead all around me, and I thought for sure I'd never get out of there alive. I was so glad to see all those boats coming in to evacuate us to England. We waded out into the water where I climbed aboard a small boat that put me back on British soil two or three hours later. I was so grateful to be alive!"

"That must have been an amazing experience," I said. What did you do after the war?"

"I came back to New England and became a contractor. I started my own business remodeling homes and, as lumber became available, my business began to thrive. I had several men working for me."

"Did you ever get married?" I asked.

"Yes, I married a girl named Margaret and we had two little daughters—Gretchie and Donna. Margaret was a wonderful wife. When I returned from work each evening she would give me a chance to rest for half an hour or so. Then she would sent Gretchie and Donna to awaken me, and we would romp around, having lots of fun before dinner. Then it happened," he said.

"What do you mean, Frank?"

"It was early March, and still quite cold. It had been snowing for almost two days. Margaret and the girls were traveling along the highway when this drunken idiot came toward them at high speed. He failed to make it around the curve and smashed into our car. In that one instant I lost my entire family!

"The jackass didn't even stay around. He dug his car out of the snow and, finding that he could still drive it, he left the scene of the accident. But he was so spaced out that he crashed into a tree farther down the highway, so the police caught him. He was sentenced to twenty years in prison and is still serving time."

"How awful! I really don't know what to say. That must have been horrible for you."

"I was so devastated by the loss of my wife and little girls that I simply walked away from my home and business and never returned," Frank said. His eyes filled with tears and he just sat there quietly for a minute or two before continuing. "For fifteen years I walked the streets filled with hatred toward that man who had robbed me of my family. I went from city to city, crossing the country. All I could think about was returning one day to take care of that drunken bastard when he got out of prison.

"And then I dropped in here at Ozanam one night. I liked it and asked for permission to stay on as a crewman. The fact that I had construction experience appealed to the administrators. So they put me in charge of a group that was renovating the Inn, mostly lowering the ceilings and installing air conditioning. So that's why I'm here now."

"That's quite a story! You must have suffered enormously over all those years," I said.

"Yes, and I'm still suffering."

I did not ask him to explain what he meant. After we had that conversation, I noticed that a long period of time went by without my seeing Frank. When I asked about him, I was told that he was in the hospital, getting ready to undergo an operation for cancer. I also learned that he had promised the Lord that, were he to survive the operation, he would, on returning to Ozanam, be baptized.

Steven and I visited him in at Charity Hospital as he prepared to undergo the operation. Before leaving him we stood on either side of his bed.

"Frank," I said, "we hope that you're not afraid."

Reaching out to grasp our hands, he turned to look at each of us.

"I'm the luckiest man in the world! Here I am at peace with the Lord, and I have two of the best friends one could ask for!"

He did indeed survive the operation and was soon afterwards baptized. A month after the operation I visited him in the crewmen's quarters at Ozanam. He was seated alone in front of a television set. On spotting me, he turned down the volume and began speaking softly.

"Deacon, I'm not going to make it," he confided.

"What do you mean? I don't understand."

"After returning from the hospital, for a while I seemed to be getting better," he related. "But not any more. Now I can feel my cancer acting up again. It's coming back and it's spreading," he explained. "I know that it's only a matter of time. A few more weeks, perhaps. A couple of months at most."

Some moments of silence followed as I struggled to think of what to say to him.

"Frank," I ventured to ask, "have you finally let go of your hatred for the man who robbed you of your family?"

"Oh, yes," he responded. "After all those years of burning with hatred toward him I finally realized that I was hurting only myself, and not him."

He paused a moment as if in deep thought. Then he gazed at me intensely.

"Deacon, he said, "when you preach, tell your people not to hate. Hatred is not good. My hatred messed up my life more than the loss of my family. That hatred ate away at my insides. I ended up hurting not the man who killed my family but myself. It was I who became the victim of my hatred!"

I saw Frank for the last time on the day before Mardi Gras when the city was jumping with merriment. Inside my coat pocket was a small metal case containing a single white consecrated wafer. Catholics refer to it as the Holy Eucharist

and believe that it is the body of Jesus the Lord. Entering
Frank's ward in Charity Hospital, I found him perspiring and
wincing in pain while grasping his abdomen. I had come to
give him a communion that was to be his last.

He informed me that he was about to be sent to a nursing facility for terminal patients in the town of Houma. I told
him that I would phone my niece Lillian, a nurse in Houma,
and ask her to visit him there. I then gave him communion.

On receiving the Eucharist he began to weep silently. I
gazed at him. "Frank, I'm sorry to see you experiencing so
much pain," I said.

He paused a moment, looked me in the eyes, and quietly
spoke. "Deacon, I'm not weeping over my pain. I want you
to know that the little white host you gave me is the best thing
that has ever happened to me! This is the happiest moment of
my life!"

After I left, while walking to my car some blocks away, it
suddenly hit me that I had witnessed something most unusual.
I had walked in on a man holding his guts in pain, knowing
that his end was near. And yet he told me emphatically it was
the happiest moment of his life. Indeed, I had witnessed a mir-
acle of the spirit and was very deeply touched by this.

Perhaps some day, during my last moments on earth, I
shall remember him, the street man who let go of his hatred
and died a very peaceful death in spite of great pain. Perhaps
the memory of Frank will one day minister to me in a special
way. I was very happy as I drove home.

"Never forget the homeless!" Frank once said. "Among
them are some of the finest people on earth!"

In Houma Lillian visited Frank. On learning that he loved
ice cream, she promised to bring him a serving on her very
next visit. A day or so later, when arriving at the nursing facility with the ice cream, she learned that Frank had just died.
Such was the hour.

In God's providence, one thing leads to another. A month
after Frank's death, I related his story in a Sunday homily

which, as it happened, was being broadcast over Loyola's powerful 50 kilowatt radio station, WWL. I explained how Frank had told me: "Tell your people not to hate! Whenever we hate, we hurt not only the ones we hate, but we also hurt ourselves!"

As I spoke, images of Frank on his deathbed entered my mind. My eyes filled up and my voice began to waver. The fact that I was being heard as far away as the Florida panhandle made it particularly embarrassing to me. Afterwards, I thought of the sermon as a failure. Certainly, it was anything but eloquent.

Days later, my feelings began to change. My pastor, to my surprise, reported that several listeners had written in, saying that they had been deeply moved by the story about Frank and had resolved to let go of their hatred. How strange are the ways of the Lord!

Gratitude

The gratitude of street people was clearly demonstrated one day as a certain man was leaving. He had stayed with us for a week and had attended our daily religious services. Before leaving the Inn, he identified himself as a Jew and a card dealer at a casino in Las Vegas. He said that he had attended our Catholic services in order to observe what went on. He told us that he was profoundly impressed by the teachings of Jesus and the ways in which they were put into action at Ozanam Inn.

Occasionally, too, a street person shows his gratitude by offering us money, usually a dollar or two. In such cases, we generally thank these people while slipping the money back into their hands. We remind them that they might be needing it more than we will. If, however, they persist, we take their offering. It is important to make a space in which people can express their generosity.

On one occasion a man wanted to make a donation. Insisting that we accept his offering, he wrote out a check to us for

$50. It bounced! The bank informed us that his account had been closed for over a year. Indeed, one might say that he was a "con man." But was he? He owed us nothing to begin with!

For the Birds

In spite of (or perhaps because of) their horrors and sorrows, the homeless seem to take refuge in things recognizably close to nature. They sometimes laugh heartily, in particular at dogs and birds. I discovered this near sundown on a memorable summer day as I ambled over to the side of the Inn. Two mockingbirds were chasing an old gray cat across the alley. A street man stood there contemplating and commenting on every phase of that melee. Meanwhile, sparrows and pigeons were beginning to arrive in search of meals.

Immediately after having gotten their sandwiches, several of the street men sat down by the side of the Inn to share their food with the birds. They ate the ham and cheese and most of the bread, then threw the crust to the birds. The men varied the sizes of the chunks of bread in order to test the capabilities of the birds. They laughed over the ways in which tiny sparrows maneuvered between the big and clumsy pigeons.

Manifesting a furious disinclination to dine with pigeons, the sparrows snatched the bread and hurriedly flew away for privacy. So heavy were certain pieces of bread—in some cases practically half the size of the tiny birds themselves—that the sparrows barely made it over the chain-link fence. Some hit the fence, momentarily held on, squeezed through the mesh with their bread, and then flew off. Others learned how to fly parallel to the fence, their tiny wings beating furiously until sufficient altitude was gained. A few paused to rest for an instant on top of the fence before taking off once more.

Strangely, the men's responses to the sparrows gave me insight into the emotional states of the men gathered there.

Like a spectrometer that receives white light and spreads it out into a rainbow of colors ranging from red to violet, the antics of the tiny birds revealed the wide range of feelings among the men. Those who were deeply depressed managed to nod a little, to smile slightly. Those who were "up" in spirit responded with cheering and laughter.

"Hey, there's my man! Look at him go!" one man shouted.

"Come on, Li'l Bit! Take it and move! Lower your flaps! Kick in the throttle, and over the fence you go!" another cheered.

It reminded me of Lindbergh taking off for Paris in his overloaded *Spirit of St. Louis*, barely clearing electric power lines at the end of the runway as people collectively held their breath!

The Joker

People called him "the Joker." His wide, infectious grin displayed only a few teeth—most of them were missing. To me, he was the archetype of toothless simplicity and I thought of him in almost universal terms. His smiles led me to look deeply within myself. Was I grinning in response to his sunny appearance? Was it because his lack of teeth had caught me by surprise? Or was it, perhaps, because of his universality? For me he seemed to epitomize a certain type of funny man reminiscent of Hollywood's Joe E. Brown from days gone by.

A big fellow with a large, bald, pumpkin-like head, he stood slouched against a wall, facing me as I walked through the third-floor dorm at Ozanam Inn.

"Hi! You come from far away?" I asked in hopes of beginning conversation.

"Well, yes and no. I stay mostly around Las Vegas, and I'm heading back there right now. I never stay in one place long. I move all over."

"Do you have a job?" I continued, chancing the question

even while knowing full well that he might respond by telling me to mind my own business.

"Not really. I once worked as a cook on an offshore drilling rig, but now they want to pay me only eight dollars an hour (this was in 1980), and I'm not about to work for less than fifteen," he said with a proud shake of his head.

"I can't help wondering how you earn your living," I said.

He leaned a little forward and grinned.

"You want me to be honest with you?" he asked in a confidential tone of voice.

"Well, of course!" I answered.

"Well, you see, I'm lazy," he said. Then he continued, "And I tell lies! And I owe people money! And all I do is travel and travel!"

"You mean you're on the run?"

"Well, ahhh, yes. I guess you could say that."

"And you have no family or home?"

"That's right. I once had a family, and I once had a fortune. I lost my family and I lost my fortune and I've been living alone for a long, long time," he said.

"You must have suffered quite a lot after losing them," I commented.

"I sure did. So, you see, now that they're gone, why should I work? I have no one to work for except myself. And I've taken care of myself just fine for years without working. So why work? I don't feel like working."

"I hear what you're saying," I said, "but if you don't mind my asking, how do you manage to pay for your food and travel?"

"Well, I hitchhike, and I make friends wherever I go. The friendliest places are the small towns. I can go directly to the police and joke with them, and they or someone they know will put me up for a night or two. And I ask people for money just like I'm going to ask you. I sometimes get $30 or $40 a day by doing just that."

"Do you like living that way?" I asked.

"Sure I do! But what does it matter whether or not I like it? There's lots of people doing jobs they don't like. I'm making ends meet, ain't I?"

"Yes, I guess you are. But, tell me, at this point in life what is it that you look forward to?" I asked.

"Nothing! I went to Texas last month hoping to die in the heat wave."

"Gosh, do you feel that bad about living?"

"I sure do. I don't have a thing in this world to live for. I have back trouble and foot trouble. I find it hard to breathe. My rear end bleeds—and it's hurting me at this moment!" he said emphatically.

"I'm very sorry about that. Sounds rough," I said. "But you also have blessings, don't you? All of us have blessings. Aren't you delighted over the fact that you can think, and talk, and whistle, and see all kinds of lovely things that can lead you to wonder about life?"

"Not really." he said. "My eyes are getting bad, so I'm a loser there, too."

"Well, what about your afterlife? Do you ever think of your possibilities for happiness after death? Aren't you looking forward to being with God in the next world?"

"No, not really."

"How do you feel about Jesus? People who are suffering often mention him. Is he someone special to you? Or is he just another man who had something a little unusual to say?" As I asked this, I realized that I was perhaps being somewhat pushy.

"Oh, I don't even think about him. Why should I?"

"Well, he had a lot to say about life, and death, and the afterlife. Don't you believe in an afterlife? Don't you believe that something of yourself will live on after your body is laid to rest in the ground?" I asked.

"No, I don't," he said emphatically. "When I die, that's the end!"

"Gosh, I hardly know what to say," I continued. "Don't you suspect that some higher Being might be interested in you at least as much as you are interested in yourself? And that this Being takes care of you by way of all those people who listen to your jokes, and give you money, and provide you with a bed on which to rest your weary bones?"

"Awww, I really don't know," he said. "I don't think like that. All I know is this: Here I am! Tomorrow I will be on the road to Vegas!"

"And what are you looking forward to on reaching Las Vegas?"

"Nothing." he said. "I owe some people money there, so I will have to be careful not to let them see me. I've got a habit of borrowing and not paying back. I sometimes joke with my lenders and they lend me more money. And I don't pay that back either!"

"Maybe the fact that they give you additional money means that they don't really expect to be paid back."

"Yeah, that's right." he responded. "That's the way that I look at it, too!"

Twenty minutes later, feeling that I had listened and said enough (and perhaps too much), I began to steer our conversation to an end. This was a man who would undoubtedly suffer very much in the future. Hopefully, someone or something down his bumpy road of pain would bring him to see more clearly that the world itself is precious because he himself, as part of the world, is of very high worth.

"Well, I've got to go now," I said. "I'll be thinking of you and praying for your safe arrival in Las Vegas. You ought to be able to get there in about a week," I said.

No way!" he exclaimed. "I don't travel like that! I might take three months to get there!"

"Well, I wish you the best, even if it takes you a year and a half to get there. And I won't forget you. I'll be thinking of you as you travel."

He extended his hand, palm upward.

"Don't ask for money," I said. "We've given you dinner and a place to sleep tonight. In the morning we'll give you a good, healthy breakfast. Aren't these worth something to you? And even if I had money to give, would it be fair to give it to you and not to the others here in this room?" I asked.

"Okay. I guess you're right," he answered, flashing a final grin.

As we parted I began to reflect on his lifestyle. Thinking about his ways of bumming a livelihood at first irritated me. Somehow it seemed unfair that he was able to get by in life begging shamelessly while others worked hard. But then I realized he probably contributed cheerfulness to those with whom he spoke. He smiled easily except when relating an instance when several young people threw objects at him from passing automobiles as he hitchhiked. Perhaps it was that which accounted for his missing teeth. I dared not ask.

While reflecting on the Joker, my mind drifted toward entertainers like Bob Hope, Johnny Carson, and Red Skelton who, in well-defined and well-controlled ways, earned their livelihoods by making people laugh. I began asking myself some questions: Why can't the Joker of Ozanam do the same? He insisted he did no work, but wasn't he in fact working? Might his work have been so natural for him that he did not think of it as work? Might he be the modern-day counterpart of the wandering minstrels of old? Who among us is not a wanderer in the sense of having no lasting home here on earth? What magic had come *my* way from this suffering, funny man who, in a sense, had stopped me in my tracks and led me to rethink certain things!

The Old Soldier

When I first met Jack, my immediate impression was that he looked as though he dated back to the era of the horse and buggy. He was a wizened old man. His skin was wrinkled and full of spots, and his toes could be seen through the cracks in his shoes. His white hair was long and disheveled, the strands hanging down like the frayed ends of half-a-dozen broken ropes. Clearly, he was caught in the grip of time. But, in spite of his diminishments, he remained friendly, warm, and jovial.

As I listened to him, I discovered he had a military past, a sergeant's rank and stories of a skirmish or two reaching back to World War II. He told about how he and his men had suffered together in military actions, how they had kept in touch over the years since their separations and retirements from the Army, how they were losing contact with one another, death being busily at work among them.

Jack was not a destitute person, for he was the recipient of a monthly military pension. He kept in touch with the Army because, as he explained, he thoroughly understood certain specialized weapons and had "heard talk" that the Army might one day seek him out for advice. When leaving Jack, I shook his trembling hand.

"I'll be praying for you," he said.

Slowly he made his way toward his bunk as if considerable reflection and full consent of the will were necessary for every move he made. His pajama bottoms, five sizes too large, slipped down his legs. He pulled them up, rolled the two front flaps into ropes of a kind, and tied them together at his waist. Gesturing toward his bunk, he said, "I'll be lying right here on this bed and praying for you and your family. Be sure to tell them that!" he added emphatically, after which he broke into a coughing frenzy as I was leaving.

An hour later I delivered Jack's message to my family. We were grateful to Jack, happy to know he was thinking of us. That was twenty or so years ago. I never saw Jack again. Almost certainly, he is no longer alive, an old soldier who had a compassionate soul and the interest of his country at heart.

Generosity

One day when I was speaking with Ozanam's administrator Steven, he had a few things to say about the generosity of street people.

"Occasionally, I meet a street person who puts me to shame in the spiritual realm with an act of patience, generosity, or compassion. I've seen street men sharing one of their last two cigarettes with another. I saw a fellow with two sandwiches give one of them to another as we were running out of sandwiches. I heard him say, 'Here, man! You can take this! I have two!' I've seen men sharing their small bottle of wine with four or five others. I do not mean to say that they needed the wine. The point I'm making is that the man with the wine understood how his street brothers felt, what it's like to want a drink and not to have one.

"Poverty tends to break down racial and cultural barriers. Surviving together draws street people closer to one another. Together they go an entire day without eating. Together they sleep outside, get wet, and are bitten by mosquitoes. They form a fraternity of a sort. I myself would trade nothing for the experience I have gained by serving them. Their humility is occasionally astounding. I am sometimes profoundly impressed by how beautifully understanding some drunken men have been on learning that we will not take in drunken persons for the night.

"'It's okay—I understand why you can't let me in,' they'll say.

"'I'm glad that you understand,' I answer. 'Try again tomorrow night. Sober up and come back. If I recognize you, I'll try real hard to find a bed for you!'

"You know, we cannot judge the state of their souls. Who really knows how strong or weak they are, or how we ourselves would fare were we in their place?

The Man Who Wore a Baby-bottle Nipple

Gathered in the chapel that evening were eight men. In came Hubert, a husky white fellow who reminded me of a wrestler. He wore a chain around his neck. It was nothing unusual, except that a rubber baby-bottle nipple hung from the chain. Two of the men already in the room spotted the nipple and looked at each other quizzically. All sat quietly while we read the biblical passage: "Blessed are the sorrowing."

While commenting on this passage, some of the men began to speak of their troubles. When Hubert's turn came and he started to speak, he got all choked up and began to weep.

"I have never felt worse in all my life!" he cried. "My wife and I buried our baby girl this morning. We tried hard to save her. We did everything we could. We took her to Charity Hospital. They tried and they tried, but she finally died. She was only five months old."

Hubert wept freely and loudly, and the men were deeply touched. I mentioned how good God was to have given his wife and him such a lovable baby; and now God wanted the baby in heaven. Hubert nodded affirmatively. When ending the session with a prayer, I mentioned Hubert and his wife in a special way. Hubert just sat there after it had ended. As the men filed out, several paused individually and placed their hand on his head or his shoulder. They whispered words of encouragement:

"I know what you're going through, Hubert! I'll pray for you!"

"Hang in there, man! Don't give up!"

Some lingered and mentioned similar experiences in their own lives. Finally, all of them left.

What had at first seemed an oddity—the wearing of a rubber nipple around one's neck—was now recognized as an expression of great sorrow, sadness over the loss of a beloved child. By means of a memento worn visibly and near to his heart, by sharing his deep human grief, Hubert was able to bring out in others their own human compassion.

"It Ain't All Over!"

Often a down-and-out person mentions the satisfaction experienced in helping others. One man of about sixty spoke in this vein.

"I've been in prison three times! I got out of the pen just two months ago. When I was in prison I would see the new young fellows coming in there. It was as if they thought their life had come to an end. They were really, really down. So I had to take them aside and tell them, 'Look, it ain't all over! You gonna get out of here some day! You must keep your head up! You must keep on going, man! You mustn't give up!'

"Well, I'm out of prison now and back on the street. I drink too much at times, mostly because there's nothing much else to do. I'm glad I'm out of prison now, but I keep on thinking about those days, and the times when I told those men to keep on trying. It makes me feel real good to think like that!"

Cutting Toenails

One never knows how a small act of kindness might touch the heart of another, and have repercussions that go far beyond the act itself.

One night, while walking through the dorm at Ozanam, I saw an elderly African-American man, bent and fatigued, sitting on the edge of his bunk with his bare feet resting on the floor. Our eyes met and we began talking. His teeth were badly discolored, and in between his statements he coughed

and coughed. With each cough, the powerful odor of stale tobacco swept over me.

Street people often have problems with their feet. The
causes of these problems are numerous, and they include ill-
fitting previously used shoes, improper diets, lack of cleanli-
ness, and simple neglect. One sometimes sees toenails
protruding half-an-inch or more in front of toes. When shoes
are too tight, they push the toenails back into the flesh and
this can cause severe inflammation. Such was the case of my
elderly tobacco-addicted coughing friend.

"Don't your feet hurt you, sir?" I asked.

"Yeah, my toes are sore. I can hardly walk because they
hurt so much."

"Looks like your nails need cutting. Would you like me to
trim them back for you?"

"All right," he replied. "Maybe that will do some good."

Kneeling on the floor, I quickly trimmed his nails and left
the scene. Minutes later another African-American man, this
one in his sixties, walked up to me with tears in his eyes.

"You know, that was a great thing you did over there,"
he said. "I was sitting across the room and I saw you cutting
that man's toenails."

"Well, I didn't think of it that way," I said. "The scissors
were handy. His toenails were long. They needed trimming.
Somebody had to do it. So I offered to cut them for him. He
was old, and I wasn't sure he could do it for himself. Also, I
don't see how cutting toenails is really so different from cutting hair or giving a man an aspirin."

"Still, I surely think that was great!"

"Well, thank you! Thank you very much, sir!" I said.

Gradually I realized that his view of this incident must
have been deeply rooted in his past. He saw it, perhaps, from
the perspective of race relations, in terms of a white man trimming a black man's toenails. Perhaps it was the first time he
had witnessed such an incident. If so, I was glad to have been
part of such a moment for him.

Amazing Compassion

Compassion implies an ability to see the problems of another as though they were happening to oneself. It is a gift that we receive to the extent that we are willing to go out of our way and identify with another. Especially with regard to the needy, compassion does not come easy, for our natural tendency is to go the other way, to identify solely with the successful, to climb aboard their bandwagons, to flow with the tides of recognition and reward. Yet compassion from others is the very ingredient needed by the unfortunate if they are to experience newness of life.

One aspect of compassion involves the ability to sympathize with those who want to speak about their hurts. In simply listening to others, we benefit from hearing about the hard-won lessons they have learned through experience while at the same time bringing them solace.

A Vietnam War veteran I once met comes to mind. He showed me scars from shrapnel on his forehead and from burns along his arms. All the scars had been acquired in combat. Pointing to the marks of his burns, he began relating a strange story of compassion. "We were fighting the Commies, and it wasn't going well, so we called for help. Soon afterwards one of our planes swooped down and dropped napalm. But the pilot miscalculated. Instead of dropping it on the enemy, he dropped it between the two sides. Both we and the enemy got napalmed!

"With the entire jungle engulfed in flames, both sides stopped shooting. We and the Commies dropped our rifles and began helping each other, throwing things on top of screaming men in order to extinguish flames and dragging each other out of that hellhole. When it ended, both the Commies and we took our wounded to ourselves. We picked up our weapons and walked off in different directions. Helicopters later evacuated us."

Tangible Signs of God's Mercy

In a world where many spend themselves in efforts to gain recognition, most street people have little desire to become great. Having made their journeys from rags to riches to rags, many are now content to live for the day at hand, and for that alone. I remind myself that there is a hidden greatness in their willingness to be ordinary in a world of many pretensions.

The lives of street people are mixtures of blessings and curses, hope and despair, wisdom and foolishness. Many of their problems stem from mental illness, addictions, sloth, poor choices, disappointments, disagreements, and emotionally impoverished childhoods. Some of these people are diamonds-in-the-rough, unwilling to be fenced in by protocol, searching for stepping stones to sobriety and newness of life.

For many, daily activities are whimsical—a visit to a bar or a park, a bull-session here or there, a pause, doing nothing, or lighting up a cigarette. Some sit and chew. They chew and talk and spit and chew. Tobacco juice hits the earth at an angle, rolls in the dust, and comes to rest beneath blades of grass. Onward goes their conversation as they voice their proclamations.

Some carry things like bottle-tops, candy wrappers, and rubber bands picked up from heaven knows where. Some are capricious, changing from sorrow to joy in an instant, hanging on to humor and trying to make each other laugh.

"I may be dumb!" one man will shout, "But I sure ain't stupid!"

Some seem to accept their plight, while others drink deeply from cups of sorrow, remaining embittered over countless "raw deals" handed to them in the past. They speak of having tried and tried and finally having lost the urge to try.

Some speak of having once worked hard for better things. They tell of their attempts to transform a life of labor into a life of leisure, of somehow having miscalculated when doing so. Engaging in high living, seeking the so-called good life, and experimenting with drugs, they set the stage for their eventual downfall. While hoping for a conjunction of events leading toward instant success, they find themselves camping in obscure forgotten places, sleeping beneath overpasses while the wheels of cars and trucks zoom by only inches above their heads.

Disenchanted over having reduced themselves to lifestyles out of harmony with their original aspirations, they navigate as if in a daze, half-asleep, half-awake. They endure their disarrayed lives under the mindless conviction that things will somehow brighten up for them without effort on their part. Thus they easily succumb to gambling, especially by playing the lotteries in hopes of instant enrichment.

How easy it is for us in our abundance to piously pray with the psalmist:

> *It is good... to make music to your name,*
>   *O Most High,*
> *To proclaim your love...*
>   *on the ten-stringed lyre and the lute. (Psalm 92)*

Indeed, it may be good for us to pray thus. However, they in their brokenness also pray with the psalmist:

> *Will the Lord reject us forever?*
> *Will he show us his favor no more?*
> *Has his love vanished forever?...*
> *Does God forget his mercy? (Psalm 77)*

I mull over this and wonder over how God's mercy might reach them. Tangible signs of God's mercy cannot come to them simply out of the blue. For us who walk the earth, compassion must visibly spring forth from ourselves and from the Spirit who works through us.

CONCLUSION

"You know, I really don't feel like going to Ozanam tonight," I sometimes say to my wife. "I've had a long day and all I feel like doing is staying here, taking an evening nap, doing a little writing, watching the news on TV, and just being with the family. I guess I'd better get going right now before I begin to feel too comfortable and start manufacturing excuses not to go!"

By the time I return home, however, my tune has usually changed.

"I'm sure glad I went to Ozanam tonight," I once said. "I met a kid tonight who was really hurting. He got into drugs. His sweetheart dropped him. His family threw him out. He stole something really big and feels that the cops are closing in on him. He imagines them to be everywhere and about to imprison him. And he is terrified at the idea of prisoners abusing him. He spoke of suicide tonight. I listened to him for a long time and gave him advice. We finally prayed together, and he was so grateful that he hugged and kissed me as I was leaving! So, I'm glad I went."

Lingering Images

Time is passing, and I am getting older. The day is coming when I will no longer be able to be of service to street people. Yet I will have them on my mind, including them with others I have known throughout my life.

When away from the homeless, I continue to picture them. I see numerous physical types—some handsome and upbeat, many plain and ordinary, a few disfigured and obviously ill.

There is one particular fellow I recall. He was big and stoop-shouldered, his hands hung low, and when I saw him I could not help thinking of a gorilla. When speaking with him, however, I was struck by his kind-hearted words.

I visualize the bald man whose skull seemed to have been cracked. The deep indentation in his cranium tells the story of a conflict or an accident. Yet he navigates the halls of Ozanam with grace and composure, smiling and talking with everyone in spite of his disfigurement.

I see the tall, thin, sunburned man who limped with a cane, and who stared into space. I see crippled fellows who obviously had been mugged, whose eyes had been blackened, whose cheeks had been bruised.

Also, I see occasional healthy-looking young men who navigate the streets, the drug addicts who go to great lengths to show how normal they are until something causes them to lose their composure, at which time they turn vicious.

I visualize the slow-moving silent and sullen ones who communicate very little. They sit staring at the floor or the sidewalk, forever waiting for time's arrow to bring them finer days that seem never to arrive. Who is to care enough to keep alive their hope? Who is to show them that they "count"?

One Redeeming Factor

I can enter their world, then leave their world. They, on the other hand, cannot do the same with respect to my world.

One cold and rainy day, an outspoken middle-aged man challenged me to talk less and go out of my way and find him a job. I made an excuse for not doing so, saying that I was far too busy with my own personal responsibilities and commitments and did not have the time to try to find employment for someone else.

"You say that you're a Christian!" he said, as he turned to walk away. "Well, I love God, too. That's easy to say, but let me see you go out of your way and really do something for me!"

Having uttered his final words he stopped, looked back, shook his head, and walked out of my life. In truth, I hated to hear those words that highlighted the gray sides of my humanity. In time I would grow to understand that he had rendered me the favor of confrontation, bringing into the light certain limitations in my ways of ministering.

No matter what we do for others, there remain areas in our work where fault can be found. And sometimes that fault is beyond our control. Perhaps, for example, had I been a religious brother, I could have gone out and found employment for someone like this man. At the time, however, I had a family with a wife and four young children as well as a full-time job with almost a hundred students to teach. Yet even when things are not beyond our control, our ministry will always be tinged by our humanity and thus less than complete. It will be limited.

We have among us the mentally ill, the alcoholics, the drug-users, the retarded, the former prisoners whom nobody will ever want to hire. Where do they go? In the context of Christian thinking wherein the Lord Jesus insisted that what we do for his least brethren we do for him, how ought we to deal with them? It's both sobering and distressing when we think of them directly in terms of Jesus walking the streets.

It is in this sense that you and I, dear reader, and the rest of humanity are poor and vulnerable. For even as we work for the Lord, we are never fully certain that we are not to some extent masquerading. Perhaps, also, vanity is at work even in persons such as I who complacently write books about street people.

But, thank goodness, there is one thing about which we can indeed be certain, one redeeming factor on which we can rely. God loves the poor—including you, my reader, and me. For everyone everywhere is poor. We all face those diminishments from which no one can escape. The homeless increase our awareness of our own limitations and, therefore, minister to us in their own ways.

As a certain religious brother once said to me, "Deacon, never forget! Many of them will be in heaven before we get there. And many of them will be waiting to greet us, holding the door open for you and me to enter."

POSTSCRIPT
GETTING INVOLVED

Much-needed improvements for street people must include better programs for the mentally ill, alcoholics, and drug-users. The enormous numbers of mentally ill people make the provision of effective help very difficult. And, when government budgets get slashed, it's the people at the bottom of the system who suffer most.

It is clear that long-range solutions are needed. But what can the average person of generous disposition do for the homeless? Shelters for street people are always in need of food, money, clothing, and personal services. It's up to individuals to determine where they might fit in as helpers. There exist huge untapped resources of people and organizations capable of providing help and support for the homeless.

Volunteers are needed for many tasks. Doctors and nurses can offer medical help one evening a week, or one afternoon a month, or whatever they can manage. Accountants can help keep financial records up-to-date. Typists can prepare letters thanking benefactors for gifts of time, talent, and treasure. Counselors for guiding the confused are especially needed, as are religious persons who can lead Bible-sharing sessions.

The poor are especially dear to God's heart. Only by getting involved can we experience the privilege of descending into their valleys and climbing their mountains, of accompanying them on their journey and so, with them, drawing closer to the Lord.